I0092611

PRAISE FOR *DISMANTLED*

"Lucidly argued and deeply researched, Dismantled gives voice to Gen-X/Millennial clergy women who have left the ministry. With a deft application of concepts of gendered scapegoating and mimetic rivalry, Horan exposes problematic social dynamics that harm clergy women. Highly recommended."

Dr. Martha J. Reineke, President of the Colloquium on
Violence and Religion (COV&R), author of
Intimate Domain: Desire, Trauma, and Mimetic Theory

"This compelling and courageous work shines a searing light on the struggles faced by Millennial clergy women navigating entrenched gender bias within American Protestantism. With profound vulnerability and incisive analysis, it unpacks the systemic issues that derail their ministries and dismantle their identities while offering a powerful call for change. Dr. Horan is a fresh voice for a new generation of leaders."

Dr. Chip Espinoza, Dean of Strategy & Innovation,
Vanguard University of Southern California,
author of Millennials Who Manage

"While scholarship has spent much time focusing on those who leave religion, far less is known about women clergy who leave ministry and the complex processes of exit. In this book, Horan innovatively examines clergy women exiting ministry as a structural gendered issue. Through careful theoretical analysis, Horan lays bare the abusive cultures that force women to leave their calling."

Dr. Sarah-Jane Page, Professor of Sociology and
Social Policy, University of Nottingham, UK, author of
Intersecting Religion and Sexuality: Sociological Perspectives

"With prophetic insight and pastoral care, Dr. Horan challenges us to confront entrenched gender and leadership norms, patriarchy, and the cultures of abuse and violence that harm Gen X and Millennial clergy women. Dismantled is one of the books that will help us take up the work of salvaging the diminished witness of the church in America."

Dr. Lewis Brogdon, Executive Director of the
Institute for Black Church Studies, BSK Theological Seminary,
author of Dying to Lead: The Disturbing Trend of Clergy Suicide

"A powerful analysis of the experience of GenX/Millennial clergy women serving as professional ministers in mainline liberal Protestant congregations. A must-read for church leaders and pastors."

Dr. Johanna W. H. van Wijk-Bos, Author of Reformed and
Feminist: A Challenge to the Church and Making Wise the
Simple: the Torah in Christian Faith and Practice

"Lynn Horan offers an unflinching account of the patriarchal dynamics that too often shape the experiences of clergy women. Interweaving narrative accounts with psychological and philosophical insight, her research offers timely guidance to women attempting to navigate the double-binds that so often accompany being female in a position of power."

Dr. Donna Ladkin, Professor of Inclusive Leadership,
University of Birmingham, UK, author of Mastering the
Ethical Dimensions in Organizations and
Rethinking Leadership

DISMANTLED

Abusive Church Culture and the
Clergy Women who Leave

Lynn M. Horan

TEHOM
CENTER

Copyright © 2025 by Lynn M. Horan

All rights reserved.

No part of this book may be reproduced in any form or by any electronic or mechanical means, including information storage and retrieval systems, without written permission from the author, except for the use of brief quotations in a book review.

Tehom Center Publishing is a 501(c)3 nonprofit publishing feminist and queer authors, with a commitment to elevate BIPOC writers. Its face and voice is Rev. Dr. Angela Yarber.

Paperback ISBN: 978-1-966655-13-8

Ebook ISBN: 978-1-966655-14-5

CONTENTS

Dedicated to clergy women who leave.

INTRODUCTION

On my last Sunday in the pulpit, I closed worship before a tear-filled congregation and then sat alone in the front pew of the 250-year-old sanctuary, my eyes gazing blankly forward. My hands retreated to a heavy stillness on my lap, having just moments before been stretched energetically outward in my final benediction as a pastor. It was World Communion Sunday, 2021, and the pews were filled for the first time since the pandemic brought communal life to a halt, yet here I sat alone with a feeling of stark emptiness preparing to publicly announce my resignation.

I intended to end my pastorate quickly and quietly, safely removing myself and my family from a small yet forceful faction of disaffected congregants, and eventually transition to a seemingly healthier congregation. I didn't know then that I was leaving ordained ministry altogether. That decision would come six months later after a highly politicized internal investigation of a church member's sexual misconduct, a mishandled severance negotiation, and the stunningly obvious yet never before mentioned fact that due to church-state separation, clergy have no legal rights in cases of work-place harassment, professional defamation, or unsafe work conditions.

I left the church a shell of myself, shattered by the ways in which my reputation had been tarnished by a handful of disgruntled parishioners and denominational gatekeepers. My family and I fled the parsonage so abruptly that I left a load of laundry in the basement washing machine and my daughter's pajamas hanging behind the bathroom door. A kind woman who was on the church board, washed the laundry herself and mailed the neatly folded clothes to me a few weeks later with a note that read, "I can't believe this happened. You were such a good pastor." As I began the painstaking process of rebuilding my life, I quickly learned that I was not alone. As I sought comradery among other clergy women who had left active ministry, I found a grieving yet grounded community of ex-clergy willing and eager to share their experiences.

Prior to my exit, I had begun a doctoral program in leadership and social change, intending to apply my interests in embodied spirituality and trauma-informed leadership to my work in congregational ministry. As I processed my own exodus, I began a pilot study exploring the interpersonal boundaries and psychological safety of Protestant clergy women. Through the participants' raw and vital testimonies, I began to see the plight of Gen-X/Millennial clergy women not as an individual tragedy to be dealt with behind closed doors, or an unfortunate mix of clashing personalities, but a systemic issue leaving younger clergy women silenced and shamed.

The initial pilot project expanded into a rigorous qualitative study including in-depth interviews with clergy women across eight Protestant denominations (Horan, 2024). The women's individual and collective experiences of feminized servanthood, psychological abuse, gendered scapegoating, and their resulting decisions to leave active ministry, are included in this book. What began as my own personal journey of recovery from toxic church culture, has become an urgent and communal call for healing, transparency, advocacy, and systemic change.

Dismantled

For Protestant clergy women who leave abusive ministry contexts, there is a distinct feeling of being dismantled. The use of the term "dismantled" is twofold as it points to the experience of being defrocked, broken down, and pushed out, but also illustrates the power one's voice and experiences have in dismantling oppressive systems. Drawn from the old French *manteler* to fortify and the Latin *mantellum* or cloak, in its most literal sense the act of dismantling means to break down the walls of a fortified building or to unravel the stitching of a garment. These images evoke elements that are organizational and structural as well as embodied and personal, which speak to the multi-layered experiences of clergy women leaving ordained ministry.

As clergy women creatively and faithfully serve their congregations, they are actively breaking down patriarchal understandings of authority and unsustainable expectations of servant-leadership. Their very presence in executive-level leadership roles is dismantling outdated and harmful church beliefs and practices. Clergy women are introducing more collaborative leadership approaches, exercising intentional decision-making, and promoting models of power-with instead of power-over that challenge prevailing gender and leadership norms. While these efforts are welcomed by most, for some the changing face of authority threatens carefully protected gender narratives and social hierarchies.

As a result of these negative perceptions, countless gifted clergy women are being rejected, targeted, and derailed, often through insidious and underhanded ways, leading to the catastrophic end of otherwise meaningful and well-regarded pastorates. The unchecked disappearance of highly-competent clergy women is dismantling the walls of American Protestantism and exposing unsustainable and harmful realities within today's churches.

Those clergy women who leave abusive churches are themselves being dismantled through chronic dehumanizing treatment, causing the fabric of one's vocational calling to fray or entirely disintegrate.

This deconstruction of pastoral identity is epitomized by the moment a woman hangs up her clergy robe for the last time. I remember zipping up my custom-tailored black cassock and neatly folding the beautifully quilted vestments, most of which were gifts from parishioners over the past decade. They were then unceremoniously sealed in a stiff garment bag as my family and I packed up our belongings from the parsonage, the pockets of my robe still laden with crumpled tissues and children's acorns from my last Sunday in the pulpit.

Some of us will wear the robe again, perhaps having found a healthier congregation or guest preaching occasionally where one is safely removed from the web of congregational conflict. Others will sell, donate, or discard their worship attire all-together, its presence symbolizing something that at one time meant so much yet no longer reflects one's evolving identity. Many will struggle for years, and some for a lifetime, with what it means to have been betrayed by an institution with which one had woven one's life, faith, and career.

Just as the act of dismantling means to dissect a piece of machinery into its component parts in order to identify its primary malfunction, the voices and testimonies included in this book offer a powerful glimpse into what has gone wrong and how it can be changed. The mass exodus of younger clergy women and the social dynamics behind their expulsion, lay bare severe structural and cultural issues within the very fabric of American Protestantism. As more women clergy draw their own lines in the sand and move beyond the corrosive patterns and engrained gender bias of even the most progressive denominations, one by one we are breaking down the façade of American Protestantism by revealing the deep-rooted conflict and intergenerational trauma that prevent the full acceptance of younger women clergy.

The Limits of Language

As a feminist researcher I am cognizant of the power of language to both liberate and oppress, and have therefore made specific choices within this body of work. A primary limitation is the distinction between the terms "female clergy" and "women clergy," as well as the overemphasis on the gender binary between men and women. I have prioritized the term "clergy women" or "women clergy," as it appropriately denotes a socially constructed gender identity that is expressed in diverse ways based on one's own lived experience. There are times when I apply the term "female" in order to offer linguistic variation, but it is important to note that "female" refers to a more fixed category of biological sex as opposed to the social identity of one's experience as a "woman." While I prefer the term "clergy woman," participants in this research also used "female clergy" to describe their experiences, which I've maintained in their interview transcripts.

In determining the most appropriate language, I recognize the obvious subordination of the terms "clergy woman" or "women's pastoral leadership," as clergy men are afforded the non-gendered identity of clergy or pastoral leader. The use of the term "clergy woman" is a firm departure from such pejorative titles as "pastor lady" or "lady pastor," which continue to be used in more culturally conservative religious contexts (Lakoff, 2004, p. 52). However, I recognize that the term "clergy woman" continues to perpetuate binary understandings of gender.

The use of binary gender language within this study (female, male, woman, man, feminine, masculine) is not reflective of the more broad and nuanced understandings of gender expressed by the research participants as well as my own feminist understanding of gender identity construction. Instead, this binary language points to the highly prescribed gender narratives within Protestant church culture, which impact surrounding perceptions of younger clergy women. The clergy women in this study navigated, resisted, and, at times, absorbed elements of these surrounding gender narratives, depending on their level of positional power and agency as well as their own individual gender identity narratives. However, it is important to clarify that gender narratives are socially constructed and the use of binary gender language does not adequately reflect the broader human and relational experience.

In addition to my deliberate choices regarding the use of gendered language, as a White race-critical researcher, I was also intentional about my use of racialized language throughout this study. Written and spoken vocabulary used to describe an individual's racial identity and thoughts and actions around racial justice is limited, and is often misinterpreted (Kendi, 2019). Moreover, racialized language can have a variety of meanings, depending on an author's purpose and personal identity, the reader's interpretation, and one's lived racialized experience. In order to acknowledge the collective and cultural identities connected to race within this study, I chose to capitalize any word or group of words representing a racial group, including Black, White, Black clergy women, White clergy women, Women of Color, and People of Color (Baker-Bell, 2020).

Navigating this Book

I began this research journey with the question: *What is the experience of Gen-X/Millennial Protestant clergy women who have left active ministry because they felt that their interpersonal and professional boundaries were violated and/or their physical or psychological safety was threatened?* This book answers that question as thoughtfully and as accurately as possibly, through rigorous qualitative research conducted through a feminist critical lens. The core data is drawn from 20 in-depth interviews with clergy women from eight different Protestant denominations, which unveiled the systemic challenges and chronic psychological abuse that the clergy women faced as they moved in, through, and beyond toxic ministry contexts.

The courageous testimonies share here revealed common themes including expectations of female servanthood, toxic masculinity, and the mother-daughter wound within congregational culture, as well as ineffective church governance, denominational complacency, and the systemic yet highly silenced phenomenon of gendered scapegoating. The staggering rise in expedited resignations of younger clergy women is a multi-layered social dynamic due to prevailing beliefs in female self-sacrifice, conflicting gender narratives, intergenerational rivalry, and a lack of legal protection for ordained clergy due to church-state separation. Through line-by-line comparative analysis of each interview, this study exposed dehumanizing and abusive elements within Protestant church culture, and the resulting loss of highly competent and intelligent Gen-X/Millennial clergy women.

This book is primarily for clergy women, including those who are entering the ministry, those who are currently serving in congregations or related ministry contexts, those who are considering leaving, and those who have already left and are in the midst of recovery. This research is also meant for denominational leaders who are aware of and deeply concerned by the pervasive targeting of younger clergy women, even within the most forward-thinking and progressive congregations. Seminary administrators, faculty, and students are also encouraged the engage in this work as it will better prepare future pastors and denominational leaders to address the intergenerational conflict and clashing gender narratives within local Protestant churches. Lastly, this book is meant for anyone who supports current and future generations of women leaders, in both religious and non-religious contexts, and those who promote more human-centered and equitable institutions where women leaders can effect positive social change.

The chapters in this book mutually inform each other in an effort to understand the lived experiences of women clergy who have left harmful ministry contexts. Chapter 1 gives an overview of the research findings, including composite narratives that paint a more visible picture of what is happening at the local church level, followed by a theoretical model that illustrates the broader social dynamics at play. Chapter 2 explores the social context of American Protestantism including elements of denominational polity and unique features of the pastor-parishioner relationship that particularly affect Gen-X/Millennial clergy women. Chapter 3 is an analysis of the philosophical underpinnings of this research, drawn from related research in the fields of feminist social theory, embodied leadership and perception, and leadership boundaries and psychological safety.

The following three chapters are a detailed analysis of the research findings, including interview excerpts and input from relevant social theories and gender critical perspectives. Chapter 4 reveals the shadow side of servant-leadership, including expectations of feminized servanthood, the mother-daughter wound, and toxic masculinity within Protestant church culture. Chapter 5 addresses the phenomenon of executive derailment through intensified psychological abuse and gendered scapegoating, and resulting decisions to leave active ministry. Chapter 6 explores the gradual process of reconstituting self, including metabolizing grief and trauma, reclaiming personal and leadership strengths, and challenging simplistic notions of reckoning and resilience having left abusive church culture.

The concluding afterword and appendix highlight the personal agency and self-actualization of clergy women who have left toxic ministry contexts or overall active ministry, and the need for institutional, cultural, and behavioral change. It is my hope that this book and the research it presents will expose the hidden and often silenced realities of Protestant clergy women whose lives are forever altered by the pain and disappointment yet also relief and liberation they have experienced in leaving ordained ministry.

PART I

FOUNDATIONS

1

DISAPPEARANCE

IN TODAY'S MAINLINE PROTESTANT CHURCHES, YOUNG women clergy navigate a precarious leadership space. While women's ordination is well-established in American Protestantism, expectations of pastoral servant-leadership, coupled with engrained gender expectations of the self-sacrificial woman, continue to present significant challenges for younger women clergy in both senior and associate-level positions. Regardless of how prophetic the preaching and compassionate the pastoral care, or how effective one is as a church administrator or community builder, today's women clergy find themselves at the crosshairs of conflicting perspectives of what it means to be a pastor, a leader, and a woman.

In the wake of traumatic resignations of even the most competent and beloved clergy women, grief-stricken congregations remain, asking, "Why did she leave?" Clergy themselves experience a deep reckoning with the religious institutions they once loved and trusted, asking, "How did this happen?" On a more personal level, women clergy are left wrestling with their own religious identity, leaving some more acutely aware of their own spiritual truths and others left desperately searching for solid ground and alternative careers outside of the ministry to which they once dedicated themselves.

Pastor-parishioner conflict is an ever-present reality for Protestant clergy due to high levels of boundary permeability within congregational church culture and reduced clerical authority in Protestant church governance. However, there is a distinct phenomenon known as "clergy killing," first outlined by Rediger (1997) with later elaboration by Maynard (2010), in which congregational conflict escalates and clergy are effectively driven out by a small group of disaffected parishioners and complacent denominational leaders. This kind of departure is in contrast to those clergy who resign on their own terms for such reasons as new job opportunities, individual or family preferences, personal health, or retirement. This study focused on those clergy women who experienced "forced resignations" (Dowding et al., 2012), having felt pushed out of their ministry contexts with no other alternative but to leave. In the wake of these painful departures, faith communities are left in a haze of confusion and blame, with clergy themselves feeling betrayed by the religious institutions they once loved and trusted.

The secular equivalent to clergy killing has been observed in related research on organizational psychology, with growing attention placed on the gendered dynamics of forced resignations and rapid turnover. Within non-religious workplace settings including corporate and business sectors, these dynamics are known as "executive or managerial derailment" (Bono et al., 2017), "push-to-leave forces" (Dwivedi et al., 2023, p. 1263), and the "glass cliff" phenomenon (Ryan & Haslam, 2005, 2007). Each of these social processes point to conflicting gender expectations and negative perceptions of women in leadership, which compromise their psychological safety and ultimately motivate their exists.

While recent business literature addresses the gendered dynamics of executive derailment, this work has not yet been applied to the experiences of Protestant women clergy. Likewise, while the work of Rediger (1997) and Maynard (2010) offer an important diagnosis of clergy killing, such analyses do not address of the plight of women clergy and their unique experiences of this often silenced dynamic. The research presented in this book integrates these two areas and reveals for the first time the gendered social dynamics that impact the executive derailment of younger clergy women and their subsequent decisions to leave active ministry. In addition, the insights and social theory drawn from this groundbreaking study can be applied to both religious and non-religious spaces as it relates to the psychological safety of women leaders.

Clergy Women in this Study

This study focused on Gen-X/Millennial clergy women, which at the time of this study were ages of 28 and 59. There were several reasons for this age criteria, including the younger ordination age of today's women clergy, intergenerational realities within predominantly Baby Boomer congregations, and the significant rise in early to mid-career attrition of younger women clergy in Protestant denominations.

The average age of women's ordination in mainline Protestant churches is 40.6 years, which is slightly older than the average age of men's ordination at 37.5 years (Hope, 2018). Among Gen-X/Millennial women clergy are those who are younger than average, having been ordained in their twenties and early thirties, as well as those who may have been ordained in their thirties and early forties and are relatively new to the ministry. Within this group, Millennial women clergy are the youngest generation of women clergy to assume high-level pastoral leadership positions in mainline Protestantism, with some securing senior and solo pastor positions in their early thirties. This is in contrast to previous generations of clergy women who typically underwent seminary training and ordination later in life, often after raising children and/or as a second career (Burnett, 2017; Page, 2016).

By focusing on this younger demographic of women clergy, this study addressed the intersectionality of gender and age and the resulting scrutiny, gender bias, and infantilization that Gen-X/Millennial women experience within their leadership roles. The term "intersectionality" points to intersecting systems of oppression including race, class, ability, sexuality, and gender, and the compounded marginalization of overlapping identities. The concept was first developed by Kimberlé Crenshaw (1989), specifically addressing the multi-layered aspects of racial and gender identity. However, Crenshaw later argued that intersectionality can be applied more broadly to any identity in which there are overlapping systems of oppression (Columbia, 2017). This study revealed that age is an important intersectional identity that intensifies already existing gender bias, whereby parishioners and denominational leaders, both men and women, seek to silence, undermine, or delegitimize the leadership of Gen-X/Millennial women clergy.

Despite the growing proportion of women graduates from Protestant seminaries (Hunter, 2016) and the increased presence of women clergy serving in solo/senior pastor leadership positions (Campbell-Reed, 2019), there has been a significant increase in early and mid-career attrition. A 2021 survey of Protestant clergy revealed that 38% of senior pastors were considering leaving the ministry. Among pastors under age 45, that number rose to 46%, with young women clergy showing the highest levels of attrition (Florer-Bixler, 2021). Some have quickly assumed that the flight of women clergy during the past few years has been largely due to pandemic-related social pressures, including work-life balance, childcare considerations, and the ongoing strain of absorbing the heightened anxiety of churchgoers as they navigated various stages of the pandemic (Gross, 2022). However, these explanations offer an overly simplistic view and fail to address systemic issues within Protestant church culture and denominational governance that cause younger women clergy to become the target of congregational conflict.

The participants in this study were those who experienced an expedited or "forced" resignation (Dowding et al., 2012), having felt compelled to leave a ministry context where their interpersonal boundaries were compromised or their psychological safety was threatened. As illustrated in business management literature (Bono et al., 2017; Dwivedi et al., 2023, Ryan & Haslam, 2005, 2007), these dynamics point to conflicting gender expectations and negative perceptions surrounding women leaders, which create an oppressive workplace environment that ultimately motivates their exists. These social processes are further pronounced among Gen-X/Millennial clergy women due to current generational dynamics within Protestant church culture, the familial nature and porous boundaries within faith-based communities, and highly gendered understandings of servant-leadership and feminized servanthood.

Composite Narratives

To illustrate the common threads within the compiled interviews, the following discussion presents two composite narratives, which honor the diverse perspectives of the research participants and at the same time highlight the systemic issues of dehumanization and psychological abuse within Protestant church culture. These narratives also include specific typologies of individuals who felt threatened by the clergy women, and were more likely to reject or criticize their leadership. A more detailed account of the research findings is presented in Chapters 4-6.

Composite narratives are meant to integrate extremely layered experiences found within qualitative interview research, yet at the same time acknowledge the complexity of the cumulative data (Willis, 2019). The following accounts weave together the varied experiences of the research participants, which ultimately represented two distinct pathways (see Table 1.1). Identified as Narrative A and Narrative B, these two representations reflect multiple women's experiences and identities, which together demonstrate a consistent landscape that the women traversed as they entered, negotiated, and eventually left Protestant church culture and pastoral ministry. It is important to note that while the women's experiences tended to fall into one of these two pathways, there was considerable overlap, particularly as the women evolved in their own leadership practice and self-understanding within their pastoral role.

Narrative A: Self-Differentiated Scapegoat	Narrative B: Driven to the Edge by Depletion
Reluctant entry into the ministry	Lifelong sense of call to the ministry
Exposure to more progressive theology promoting social justice and equality	Exposure to more conservative theology promoting self-sacrifice and humility
Entered the ministry in mid-thirties with prior professional experience	Entered the ministry in mid-twenties with exclusively ministry experience
Held solo/senior pastor and head-of-staff positions	Held associate pastor or youth/family ministry positions
Ability to self-differentiate and establish boundaries around pastoral role due to executive level position	Less ability to self-differentiate and maintain boundaries due to reduced positional power
More financial security and ability to leave amid congregational conflict	Less financial security and ability to leave amid congregational conflict
Primary leadership approach: decisive, addressing conflict directly, engaging positional power when needed	Primary leadership approach: relational, smoothing over conflict, securing trusted allies due to limited positional power
Leadership ethos: collaborative, mutual accountability, shared knowledge, emotional intelligence	Leadership ethos: collaborative, mutual accountability, shared knowledge, emotional intelligence
Primary dehumanizing social dynamic: escalated scapegoating led by small group of disaffected parishioners with rigid gender expectations	Primary dehumanizing social dynamic: ongoing psychological abuse from toxic senior pastor and complicit church/denominational leaders
Recovery process: Self-doubt in leadership ability, "What did I do wrong?", disconnecting from religion	Recovery process: Emotional and physical depletion, "Am I the worst?", wrestling with personal faith

Table 1.1: Composite Narratives A and B

NARRATIVE A: SELF-DIFFERENTIATED SCAPEGOAT

Woman A was loosely affiliated with a Protestant denomination throughout her life but had pursued other professional paths prior to ordained ministry, primarily in non-profit community development. Entering the ministry was not initially on her radar, but her passion for community-building alongside a deep sense of spiritual curiosity eventually brought her to a three-year graduate program at a Protestant seminary. She resonated with the seminary's progressive theology and community ethos and felt her leadership skills were well-suited for congregational ministry, particularly with her ability to build relationships within multigenerational settings as well as her expertise in conflict resolution and complex problem-solving.

Based on her significant prior professional experience, Woman A was a much sought-after pastoral candidate and was quickly hired as the solo pastor of a large congregation, where she oversaw other church staff and a variety of programmatic areas. Throughout Woman

A's ministry, she was intentional about establishing boundaries around her pastoral role and time availability, particularly after starting a family. As the first woman to hold this position, she began to notice resistance from a few congregants who were accustomed to previous male pastors' constant availability and willingness to involve their families in all areas of church life. Parishioners' anxiety regarding pastoral accessibility was further heightened due to denominational policy changes that required local churches to include maternity leave policies and limit pastoral contracts to a 40-hour workweek.

After a few years, Woman A moved to her second solo pastor position where the congregation expressed excitement about hiring a woman pastor who was also the mother of young children. However, Woman A quickly found that a few older women questioned her decision to limit her children's involvement in the church and her inability to attend certain evening committee meetings due to her partner's job schedule. Woman A eventually had a conversation with one of the women, asking directly whether she had offended someone and whether there was anything she could do heal whatever rift existed between her and this group of older women. The woman parishioner shared that people generally thought that Woman A "wasn't pastoral enough" and that she needed to be more present at the church on the weekends and visit more people in the hospital.

Woman A tried to embrace the comments as constructive criticism yet at the same time felt that her intense administrative responsibilities and weekly preaching made it such that she could only make a few pastoral-care visits a week and Saturdays would remain a personal day for her family. The pushback continued and she started to feel that she was never going to be enough or do enough to satisfy the congregation's varied needs and that others' expectations of her were becoming unsustainable.

In an effort to develop alternative ministry models that would support the needs of the congregation, Woman A scheduled a special meeting with the church board to explore the possibility of merging with another local church that was struggling to afford their part-time pastor. The woman who had previously confronted Woman A about her availability for pastoral-care needs used the incident to create an incriminating narrative that framed Woman A as a divisive figure in the community, eager to dismantle the church's commitment to family values and unwilling to care for the most vulnerable parishioners. At the same meeting, a male congregant who was the head of the building and grounds committee accused Woman A of misusing the property by allowing "politicized community groups" to hold occasional meetings at the church, despite the decision having been approved by the church board. A handful of others at the board meeting sat quietly as the criticism escalated, yet they were visibly stunned by the accusations that were being made. Woman A maintained her composure, calmly receiving the feedback during the meeting, despite feeling completely annihilated by a community that she had grown to deeply care for.

Over the next few months, commentary began to build around others' perceptions of Woman A's dishonest intentions and incompetence as a leader. While she tried to remain grounded and focused on her pastoral responsibilities, she felt unable to defend herself amid the growing distrust surrounding her leadership. She contacted a retired clergy colleague who had become a mentor to her and described the dynamics she was observing. He was genuinely sympathetic of her plight, noting that this was not the first time he had seen this happen, and ultimately advised her to quietly leave and look for an alternative pastoral position in a healthier congregation.

Over the next few weeks, Woman A began looking for a new position and made several strategic steps to resign quietly and with dignity. However, the surrounding spiral of anxiety and blame quickly gained momentum as the small group of disaffected parishioners began to actively scapegoat Woman A in ways that she was completely unprepared for. The male groundskeeper who had initially voiced frustration over what he felt was inappropriate use of the building, met with a few other congregants privately. The group ended up drafting a letter of complaint to the denomination, recommending her removal on the grounds that Woman A was aggressive and controlling and was taking away their voice in church decision-making. In a similar effort to corral others against Woman A, the older woman who had previously expressed frustration over Woman A's insufficient pastoral-care visits and intentional boundaries around her family, ended up pressuring several other women to withdraw their membership from the congregation in protest of Woman A's lack of respect for "the way things have always been done."

While Woman A was aware of the dissatisfaction among certain parishioners, she felt completely blindsided by the fury of events happening around her as more and more congregants became swept up in a whirlwind of character defamation against her. Having held significant leadership positions in other professional sectors, she had never experienced this kind of targeting and control of a single narrative, which she felt did not represent who she was as a person or as a leader. After contacting a denominational representative, she was told there was "nothing they could do," despite having been aware of the growing conflict for months. She was shown the letter of complaint drafted by her most vocal opponents, which for her was the "nail in the coffin."

Feeling completely isolated and at a loss of allies in her local congregation, it was at this point that Woman A expedited her resignation plans. While it wasn't ideal, Woman A and her spouse felt they could afford her loss of income if she resigned without having alternative employment in place. She no longer felt she could effectively lead a congregation that had lost faith in her as a leader, even if it was only a small contingent of adversaries. Despite her efforts to build a sustainable community using effective models of ministry and community engagement, Woman A felt her leadership and presence was no longer welcome or valued.

On her final Sunday, preaching before a congregation she felt like she no longer knew, Woman A wondered if it was worth it to have entered the ministry in the first place, knowing it would end in this way. She was horrified by the level of vitriol that swept through the congregation, including people who had consistently affirmed her leadership over the past few years. She felt comfort and validation from several members of the surrounding community who had seen her as a highly respected, bridge-building leader. She publicly communicated that she was voluntarily resigning, but in reality, she felt pushed out by a small but powerful contingent of congregants and complacent denominational leaders.

It took Woman A longer than she expected to recover from the intensity of events that centered around her in those final months. The level of discord concerning her pastoral leadership and personal identity caused her to deeply question the relational bonds that she had built during her time in ministry, as well as evaluate her own competence as a leader. She asked herself for months, "What did I do wrong? Could I have changed the outcome in any way? What was so horrible about my leadership that created such angry opposition?" At the same time, she knew that she had been a highly effective and compassionate leader, with several church members and denominational leaders contacting her in the months following her departure acknowledging how unhealthy the congregation was, and feeling sorry that they didn't do more to support her.

A meager severance afforded Woman A a few months to heal and recover, during which she considered taking a position in a healthier ministry context, but a gut feeling told her to not to pursue it. She ultimately identified feelings of betrayal, having felt that the system she had entered would never fully embrace her identity as a woman leader, particularly one that exhibited healthy boundaries around her personal life and pastoral role. She ultimately decided that she was not willing to fit into a mold that denied her humanity and her understanding of shared communal responsibility and accountability. While she held onto certain core understandings of faith and theology that continued to be important to her, Woman A ultimately decided to disengage both personally and professionally from organized religion.

After four years of processing the grief and sadness of leaving ordained ministry, Woman A has come to terms with how her ministry ended and is now thriving in an adjacent career as a university social worker. She is grateful for the opportunity to apply her pastoral care skills and awareness of interpersonal dynamics, as well as being vigilant of harmful gender narratives that effect women, in particular the women college students that she sees in her new line of work. Looking back, she's grateful she "got out" when she did, even if it wasn't entirely on her terms. She is now extremely proud of how she has reclaimed her identity and her leadership abilities in ways that have been life-giving.

NARRATIVE B: DRIVEN TO THE EDGE BY DEPLETION

Women B felt a call to ministry at an early age, having been steeped in the Protestant tradition throughout her upbringing and having received positive mentoring from an older clergy woman in her local church. During seminary she reevaluated the more conservative theologies to which she had been exposed and felt prepared to enter the ministry with a deep commitment to social justice and inclusive leadership practices. Having entered the ministry in her mid-twenties, she started as an associate pastor in a large multi-staff church, where she oversaw youth and family ministries. She enjoyed the work of building strong bonds with younger families as well as honing her collaborative leadership skills grounded in empowering others and bringing more voices to the table.

As Woman B's popularity grew within the congregation, with her team-oriented leadership style being well-received by others, the male senior pastor became confrontational, often publicly shaming or blaming Woman B for conflict within the church. Woman B began to endure significant emotional abuse, including harsh criticism of her work that reached a high point as the pastor underwent a difficult divorce. Women B felt like she was the punching bag for all of his emotional insecurities and turmoil within his family. Despite others in the congregation recognizing the senior pastor's harmful treat-ment, there was a general consensus that the male pastor's charis-matic leadership was needed in order for the congregation to survive financially. As a young single woman, Woman B felt trapped as she needed to keep her employment and health benefits. She was not in a position to leave the church without alternative employment in place. Moreover, she felt deeply committed to her call to ministry and wondered whether dealing with toxic leaders was simply part of the job.

Woman B struggled for months with what to do, seeking counsel from other pastors and colleagues, many of whom said, "I'm so sorry this is happening to you, but this is just a part of the job." Fortunately, Woman B had been seeing a therapist who was aware of the psychological abuse she was experiencing. The therapist asked a simple question that hit a strong chord for Woman B, "Are you happy or are you hurting?" Woman B immediately burst into tears, having not yet acknowledged the intense physical and emotional toll of working in such a dehumanizing environment. Her own response was just as striking, "I didn't know that I was allowed to be happy."

In that moment, Woman B made a profound connection with her own mother's experience as a single mother, working multiple jobs to provide for her children. She had never seen her mother take time for herself or ask herself what she wanted. Woman B realized that she had absorbed her mother's experience in a way that was now harming her. Upon deeper reflection, Woman B also identified a past history of domestic violence, in which her biological father had periodically returned only to blame her mother for not doing enough. Recalling these memories was incredibly painful for Woman B, but she ultimately began to see parallels between her mother's experience in an abusive relationship and the larger church system. It felt like a catch-22 in which those who praised her as a model of Christian service were just as willing to demolish her for wanting to be simply treated as a human.

As Woman B tried to find alternative employment as a pastor while still enduring the psychological abuse at the church, she hit rock bottom. After complaining of stomach pains for several weeks, her doctor informed her that she had developed a stress-induced condition that would require immediate surgery. A few church members sent a bouquet of flowers to the hospital with the note, "Hurry back, we miss you!" Woman B felt a strong feeling of disgust as if being lured back into an abusive relationship. Once she returned home, she called a denominational representative and requested extended medical leave based on her doctor's recommendation. She underwent several days of negotiation in order to secure three weeks paid medical leave, which was already part of her employment contract. Such resistance to fair employment practices further alerted Woman B to the ways in which the denominational system promoted an unhealthy model of service and sacrifice, particularly for younger clergy women.

Woman B was unable to secure paid medical leave and instead used three weeks of accumulated sick leave and vacation time, which she never felt that she could use while she was working. During her recovery period, she unceremoniously resigned and never returned to the church. She realized over time that she had absorbed a damaging ethos of martyrdom, to the point that she didn't feel she could use her allotted paid time off or invest in her own emotional well-being despite offering such support to others. Through ongoing therapy, she realized that her sense of self-worth had deteriorated due to harmful theologies of humility and habitual people-pleasing.

She eventually shared her experience with her own mother, and together they recognized some of the trauma that had been passed down between generations, in which the women in their family had selflessly served others at the expense of their own physical and emotional needs. In addition to unpacking her own personal family history, Woman B began a long journey of rewriting narratives based on "bearing one's cross" that had reinforced some of the dehumanizing gender narratives that she had absorbed.

It took Woman B two years before stepping back into a church, and even when she did, she questioned whether she indeed belonged there. She considers herself in a place of spiritual exploration, as she acknowledges that the foundations of faith on which she had built her life and vocation eventually led to personal harm and denial of self. Having moved to another state, Woman B started a new job at a local book store where she continues to heal. She feels relieved to no longer be expected to "be nice" at all costs or to absorb others' emotions, particularly from people who are actively hurting her. She also enjoys being able to close up the shop at the end of the day, and not bring work home or be expected to be constantly available. She's grateful that she left ordained ministry when she did, before she lost herself completely. Woman B is not sure where her life will lead her, but she's becoming more comfortable with that uncertainty as she attends to her own wants and needs.

Examined together, Narrative A and Narrative B reflect overlapping layers of experience shared by the research participants. Overall, the composite narratives reflect two pathways that emerged in the data: 1) a highly self-differentiated clergy woman who was publicly shamed and eliminated through the process of gendered scapegoating and 2) a clergy woman with a strong sense of vocational calling and internalized messages of female self-sacrifice, who was driven to the edge by psychological abuse and physical depletion. These two trajectories are not mutually exclusive and instead overlap considerably, with most of the participants experiencing a combination of both the dehumanizing process of scapegoating as well as chronic exposure to psychological abuse. Also evident throughout both paths were instances where the clergy woman exercised self-actualization and agency, which was often met with others' intensified scapegoating behaviors and/or psychological abuse.

As illustrated by the two composite narratives, the overall chronology of the women's experiences in, through, and beyond abusive ministry settings included 1) a sense of being called or drawn into the ministry; 2) negotiating dehumanizing expectations of feminized servanthood; 3) exercising leadership strengths and varying levels of self-differentiation; 4) intensification of psychological abuse and/or scapegoating behaviors; and 5) an expedited departure or forced resignation from a pastoral leadership position due to gendered scapegoating or physical and/or psychological depletion.

WHAT ALL IS HAPPENING HERE?

In the words of sociologist Leonard Schatzman (1991), I approached this research with the central question, "What all is going on here?"

Through rigorous qualitative study, I sought to explore an unaddressed social phenomenon and reveal what is happening beneath the surface within Protestant church culture. In conducting this study, I wanted to offer for myself and others the opportunity to think about "whether this is the world we wanted to create, and if not, what would be our alternative proposal" (Lincoln and Guba 2013, p. 10). It was this desire to uncover what has been systematically hidden and silenced that guided this research and my own interpretive lens.

Drawn from line-by-line comparative analysis of verbatim interviews, the following diagram (Figure 1.1) illustrates the primary social dynamics that influence the executive derailment and subsequent disappearance of Gen-X/Millennial Protestant clergy women (Horan, 2024). A more detailed examination of these research findings is discussed in Chapters 4-6.

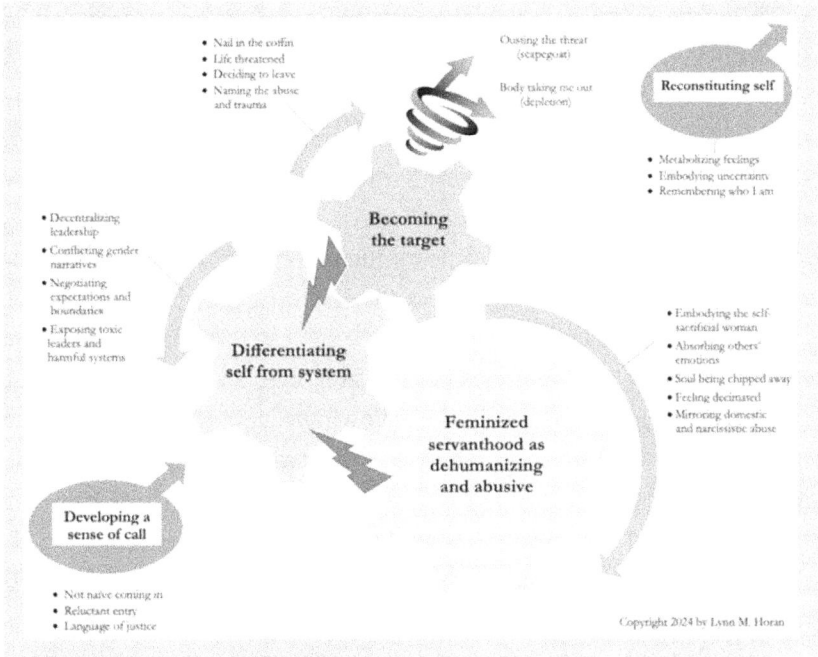

Figure 1.1: Feminized Servanthood, Gendered Scapegoating, and the Disappearance of Gen-X/Millennial Clergy Women

The central feature of this visual is a rotating gear mechanism with key tension points representing the highly pressurized and conflictual social dynamics of Protestant church culture. In order to function, a system of gears requires a specific relational orientation. Similarly, the congregational conflict experienced by the clergy women in this study was the result of specific relational processes that built off of each other in compounded ways. There is also potential for added friction between the rotating gears, exhibited by electrical charges, which depict increased system anxiety when the clergy women exhibited varying levels of self-differentiation. While the use of the gear metaphor is helpful in visualizing the social processes that took place in each of the women's ministry settings, it is important to reinforce the multi-layered, human-centered nature of this study, as opposed to a mechanical or one-dimensional understanding of the social processes at play.

The three gears represent the primary social dynamics revealed in this study, which included 1) *feminized servanthood as dehumanizing and abusive;* 2) *differentiating self from system;* and 3) *becoming the target.* These three components were drawn from the research participants' own individual language and meaning-making processes, followed by comparative analysis of the overall interview content. The opposing directions of each of the three gears illustrates the tension and resistance experienced by the women as they negotiated conflicting gender narratives and exhibited varying levels of agency. Each of the gears has a cluster of corresponding conceptual categories and social processes, which are developed further in the following chapters. Spiraling out of the final gear of *becoming a target* are the two primary mechanisms through which the women left their ministry contexts. These two exit points are *ousting the threat (scapegoat)* and *body taking me out (depletion),* which were outlined respectively in the composite narratives A and B noted above (see Table 1.1).

Following the dramatic expulsion or debilitating withdrawal from their ministry contexts, each of the women underwent a painstaking process of recovery, denoted by the category of *reconstituting self* in the upper right corner of the visual model. This experience includes the ongoing social processes of metabolizing feelings of betrayal and shame, embodying the uncertainty of one's identities and vocational calling, and gradually reclaiming a sense of self that was lost or compromised while in active ministry. While the women exhibited important self-actualization and agency while still engaged in pastoral leadership, the process of reconstituting self grew in clarity and intensity once the women had left their respective congregational social systems.

The clergy women's experiences of recovery are ongoing and nonlinear, and continue to evolve in important and complex ways. The painstaking process of recovery does not have a fixed endpoint (Aranda et al., 2012) and should not be oversimplified as the inevitable character-building work of overcoming hardship (Gill & Orgad, 2018). Such one-dimensional understandings of resilience are harmful, as they place the onus on survivors to absorb structural oppression as a necessary element of their own self-realization, rather than critically examining the dehumanizing conditions that necessitated such recovery of self (Roberts, 2022, p. 186). As will be discussed in Chapter 6, these realities warrant further longitudinal study, particularly as it relates to religious trauma, psychological abuse, institutional betrayal, and the ongoing recalibration of one's life in relation to self and community.

2

SOCIAL CONTEXT

Despite the long-standing history of women's ordination in American Protestantism, there are engrained cultural beliefs and practices that directly and indirectly undermine women's pastoral leadership. Within this more progressive religious context, insidious elements of gender bias are harder to identify than the overt discriminatory behavior and denominational policy of more conservative religious institutions that resist or reject efforts to ordain and employ women clergy (Page, 2016; Roberts, 2016; Rocca, 2023). The tacit social dynamics and conflicting gender narratives within American Protestantism severely impact the interpersonal boundaries and psychological safety of Gen-X/Millennial clergy women, leading to a significant rise in younger clergy women leaving active ministry.

Within mainline American Protestantism, there are specific historical, relational, and structural realities that contribute to the executive derailment of Gen-X/Millennial clergy women. Outlined in Table 2.1, these concepts include: 1) long-standing male hetero-normativity of pastoral leadership; 2) historical anxiety surrounding women's leadership and the female body; 3) younger age of women's ordination and access to senior-level positions; 4) conflicting gender identity narratives; 5) intergenerational dynamics between younger clergy and largely Baby Boomer congregations; 6) increased clergy boundary-setting around the pastoral role; 7) increased polarization and high boundary permeability within congregational culture; 8) insufficient training of volunteer HR committees; and 9) reduced clerical authority and lack of secular legal representation for clergy. It is important to note that these dynamics are not exhaustive and may not capture specific underlying realities within individual congregations and pastor-parishioner relationships. However, they do provide a framework for addressing the abusive and dehumanizing treatment of younger clergy women in today's Protestant churches.

Historical	Relational	Structural
Longstanding male hetero-normativity of pastoral leadership	Conflicting gender identity narratives	Increased polarization and high boundary permeability within congregational culture
Historical anxiety over women's leadership and the female body	Intergenerational dynamics between young clergy and largely Baby Boomer congregations	Insufficient training of volunteer HR committees
Younger age of women's ordination and access to senior level positions	Increased clergy boundary-setting around pastoral role	Reduced clerical authority and lack of secular legal representation for clergy

Table 2.1: Contributing Factors to the Rise in Clergy Women Attrition

HISTORICAL

Mainline American Protestantism is generally understood to be a more progressive and change-oriented branch of Western Christianity, due to its historical commitment to representative governance, reduced clerical authority, rigorous scholarly inquiry, and acceptance of non-literal interpretation of biblical text. Such openness to social change through Reformed theology and democratic decision-making has resulted in important denominational policies that are supportive of gender equality, followed by certain denominations affirming reproductive rights, same-sex marriage, and the ordination of LGBTQ+ clergy (Smith, 2015; Youngs, 2011). Starting with the Presbyterian Church (USA) in 1956, women's ordination has become largely accepted throughout mainline Protestantism, leading to a significant rise in women seminary graduates and ordained clergy women serving throughout congregational and denominational leadership (Burnett, 2017).

Women clergy account for a third of seminary students, the highest percentage in history (Miller, 2013), with fully credentialed women clergy rising from below 10% in 1977 to between 20% and 40% in 2017, depending on the denomination (Campbell-Reed, 2019, p. 33). However, despite these significant advancements, barriers to the full acceptance of women clergy continue to exist within mainline Protestantism, where only 10% of senior and solo pastor positions are held by women (Barna, 2019). This percentage drops significantly by age, with senior-level women clergy under the age of 45 years considered extremely rare.

While these historical shifts have resulted in new generations of clergy women entering ordained ministry, local congregations and governing structures are still highly characterized by patriarchal, bureaucratic, and male-centered leadership models, which present significant barriers to the full expression of women's pastoral leadership (Bendroth, 2022; Campbell-Reed, 2019; Rohrer, 2020). Even as progressive Protestant congregations seek to promote social justice in concrete church programs and community outreach efforts, local church culture continues to absorb surrounding patriarchal social norms, behaviors, and beliefs that scrutinize the female body and women's pastoral leadership (Torjesen, 1993; van Wijk-Bos, 2022).

While the strong intellectualism of the Protestant tradition has promoted social equality and the general acceptance of women clergy, the more cognitive and cerebral nature of mainline Protestantism has created a distinctly disembodied religious expression. Theologian Marcia Mount Shoop (2010) noted that understandings of embodied experience within Christian belief and practice are often limited to lessons on self-control and moderation. She described the "Protestant problem" in which "our bodies have been seen as a liability, a conspirator in our fallenness. . . . We live in a Christian community with only a thin layer of understanding of our own embodied capacity to experience redemption" (pp. 2, 11). While the Reformed tradition has expansive understandings of incarnational theology, the rejection of the physical body in local church teachings and faith practices fail to embrace the fullness of the human experience, particularly as it relates to engrained beliefs and subconscious assumptions regarding race, gender, and sexuality. This theological and historical context has created a deeply fraught leadership space for today's younger clergy women, who often become the target of congregations' conflicting world views and theological outlooks.

RELATIONAL

Conflicting Gender Narratives

Gen-X/Millennial clergy women who are employed as senior and solo pastors are oftentimes the first or second woman to hold such a position in a congregation's leadership history. This lack of gender parity and the perceived uniqueness of seeing a younger women clergy in an executive-level role, creates a sense of heightened visibility (O'Neill, 2018), where one's leadership, physical presence, and overall way of being is constantly surveilled. Known as "gender role congruency" (Eagly & Karau, 2002), parishioners and other church leaders relentlessly, yet often unconsciously, assess whether a clergy woman measures up to one's idealized understanding of what it means to be a pastor and a woman.

While a clergy woman's "otherness" can carry a certain appeal or novelty at first, such initial acceptance is often based on essentialist understandings of women leaders. To essentialize means to characterize a quality or trait as fundamental or intrinsic to a particular type of person or thing. Employers can essentialize women as more relational or agreeable, leading to harmful expectations that women leaders quell or absorb institutional conflict (Marrone, 2018; Ryan & Haslam, 2005, 2007). Such engrained gender expectations cause women leaders who exhibit healthy boundaries, agency, and decisive leadership skills to be viewed more critically, in ways that their male counterparts may not experience.

While congregations may initially respond with acceptance and enthusiasm toward a clergy woman, parishioners may eventually perceive particular qualities or approaches within her pastoral leadership to be in conflict with established gender norms and preferred notions of "mainline masculinity" (Bendroth, 2022, p. 98). This places younger clergy women in a "double-bind" (Tanner, 2016), where they are expected to perform their gender through binary notions of feminized relationality, which some may criticize as soft or ineffective leadership. At the same time, a more assertive or agentic leadership approach may be considered incongruent with gender role expectations of compliance and agreeability. Tanner (2016) outlined this "double bind" by noting the persistent binary qualities that continue to restrict women in leadership positions:

> A double bind means you must obey two commands, but anything you do to fulfill one violates the other. While the requirements of a good leader and a good man are similar, the requirements of a good leader and a good woman are mutually exclusive. A good leader must be tough, but a good woman must not be. A good woman must be self-deprecating, but a good leader must not be.

Qualitative research on women clergy in American Protestantism has expanded significantly over the past 30 years due to the comprehensive work of Zikmund et al. (1998), as well as more recent studies that have tracked the changing dynamics of women in ordained ministry (Burnett, 2017; Campbell-Reed, 2019). Also influential was the inclusion of women clergy as ordained priests in the Church of England in 1992, which has brought important ethnographic and case study research from British and Australian leadership scholars exploring clergy women pastoral identity (Roberts, 2016), vocational calling and work-family balance (Greene & Robbins, 2015; Page,

2016), and compassion fatigue and emotional burnout (Frame & Shehan, 2004; Myers, 2020).

While research in these areas apply an increasingly feminist critical lens, there is a tendency to place the onus on women clergy themselves to increase strategies of self-care and work-life balance, rather than addressing overarching systems of oppression that reject clergy women boundaries and agentic leadership. The current emphasis on individualized coping mechanisms for women leaders is also evident in similar community-oriented professions such as counseling (Burke, 2022), collegiate student affairs (McKinney, 2022), and school superintendency (Polka et al., 2008). In addition to these more surface-level solutions, current research also fails to address the more nuanced interpersonal work of boundary-setting and the resulting push-back that more self-differentiated clergy women leaders experience when implementing these strategies.

The Pastor-Parishioner Relationship

As ordained clergy move between an array of roles, job responsibilities, and relational expectations, parishioner perceptions of their pastoral leaders can vary significantly. Beyond the performativity of the clerical robe and positional power of the pulpit and sacramental rituals, the identity of the individual pastor operates in a complicated way based on the individual psychological needs of the parishioner.

Sociologist Steven Reiss (2015) argued that individuals participate in spiritual or faith-based communities, consciously or unconsciously, due to unmet human identity needs, which an individual hopes the faith community and/or pastor can fulfill. Reiss observed 16 basic human desires that motivate engagement in religious communities, including power, independence, curiosity, acceptance, order, saving, honor, idealism, social contact, family, status, vengeance, romance, physical activity, and tranquility (p. 17). These desires can often be manifested in individuals with opposite personality traits, leading to intense polarization and emotional projection within local church culture. What further complicates the pastor-parishioner relationship is when the pastor's own identity becomes the site where parishioners' conflicting psychological needs are negotiated.

A parishioner's understanding and acceptance of who the pastor is, both as a person and as a leader, are highly dependent on the particular needs, wants, and desires of the parishioner and the role one expects the pastor to play in one's life (Redekop, 2002). If the perception of the pastor's personhood does not align with the role desired by the parishioner, there is a direct link to the parishioner's inability to trust, follow, accept and/or respect the pastor. This misalignment between pastor and parishioner expectations intensifies when it comes to self-differentiated clergy women, whose very presence and way of being can disrupt long-held beliefs and societal norms of the compliant and self-sacrificial woman.

Intergenerational Conflict

The generational realities of today's Protestant churches reveal another layer of relational friction, particularly when it comes to conflicting gender identity narratives of Gen-X/Millennial women clergy and their largely Baby Boomer congregants. A striking disconnect is evident between Gen-X/Millennial clergy women and Baby Boomer women, who represent the largest demographic of mainline Protestant parishioners (Public Religion, 2020). Tension between these two generations of women is often due to internalized sexism among certain older women who have been denied agency in their own lives, causing them to question or resent the increased social mobility and positional power of younger women leaders (Hasseldine, 2017).

Conflicting gender narratives between women in secular workplace settings has gained attention within business management scholarship (Ellemers et al., 2012; Marrone, 2018; Ryan & Haslam, 2005, 2007). However, there are specific intergenerational tensions that exist within Protestant Church culture, due to the familial nature and boundary permeability of the pastor-parishioner relationship, particularly between Gen-X/Millennial clergy women and certain Baby Boomer women parishioners and church leaders. As will be discussed further in Chapter 4, this study revealed a pervasive mother-daughter wound where older women's expectations of what it means to be a woman and a pastor severely compromise the interpersonal boundaries and psychological safety of younger clergy women.

Increased Boundary Setting

Due to younger ordination age and quicker ascension to senior leadership positions, today's young women clergy are introducing new realities to the pastoral role. Gen-X/Millennial clergy, regardless of gender, are promoting alternative ministry models to the corporate and capitalistic models of parish ministry that were prevalent in previous generations of male-centered pastoral leadership (Rohrer, 2020). In addition to changes in leadership philosophy and practice, younger clergy women are also presenting new familial realities, which older congregants may not have encountered with previous pastors.

Gen-X/Millennial clergy women are often the first pastors in their congregation's history to introduce maternity leave policies or negotiate family leave allowances due to overlapping caretaker roles (Page, 2016). In addition, today's young clergy women are often part of a bivocational family, with full-time working spouses or partners who are not necessarily engaged in parish culture. This is in contrast to previous generations of male-centered pastoral leadership, where clergy wives were highly involved in uncompensated church leadership (Frame & Shehan, 2004; Roberts, 2016).

American Protestantism has historically featured male-centered expressions of pastoral leadership that promote solo achievement and capitalistic stakeholder models of productivity. This has created unrealistic expectations of a pastor's constant availability and lack of boundaries around the pastoral role (Rohrer, 2020). However, this mythical notion of a pastor's constant presence has largely been possible due to behind-the-scenes, unpaid spousal support that enables male pastors more time, freedom, and availability to ensure the needs of the larger congregation. As a result of this inivisibilized work, an unspoken expectation often placed on today's younger clergy women is that they take on both the role of pastor and clergy spouse, which has been historically fulfilled and/or imposed on the wives of male clergy (Greene & Robbins, 2015). Today's younger clergy women are often expected to uphold the dual roles of the constantly available pastor and ever-present clergy spouse, in ways that are unsustainable and discriminatory.

The expectation of unchecked availability has proven to be unhealthy and unrealistic for pastors, their families, and their congregations, resulting in important denominational policy changes including a 40-hour work week and requirements for paid vacation, continuing education, family leave and, more recently, maternity leave (Office of the General Assembly, 2021). However, despite more standardized professional contracts, gendered expectations of the compliant and conciliatory woman continue to exist, which pressure younger clergy women to perform above and beyond the call of pastoral leadership (Greene & Robbins, 2015).

The increased alterity or otherness of women clergy has strong implications for what Greene and Robbins (2015) described as "sacrificial embrace," in which clergy override feelings of psychological stress due strong vocational commitment. While this dynamic is felt by clergy regardless of gender, the acceptance of such sacrifices has more direct and damaging consequences for clergy women within the gendered context of congregational life (p. 408). Cultural expectations of the self-sacrificial woman coupled with a pastor's deep sense of calling, place younger clergy women at risk of accepting unsustainable levels of boundary crossing, harassment, and unrealistic job requirements as compared to their male clergy counterparts. For those clergy with less positional power, financial flexibility, or job security, absorbing these excessive expectations leads to extreme emotional and physical burnout. For those who exhibit strong boundaries around the pastoral role and resist some of the gendered expectations of self-sacrifice, there is significant pushback, including systemic bullying, targeting, and scapegoating of younger clergy women who do not comply (see Table 1.1. above). Both cases lead to dehumanizing and abusive treatment, with some clergy women having more agency and ability to leave than others.

STRUCTURAL

Polarization and Boundary Permeability

Based on the collective decision-making approaches and limited clerical authority within Protestant church governance, today's Protestant clergy are trained to be extremely competent at systems-level thinking in order to enhance productive conflict resolution (Gray & Tucker, 2022). However, local and regional church governance is often stifled by ineffective decision-making where binary opposition or oversimplified uniformity impede the development of new perspectives. The emergence of integrative polarity work in organizational and adaptive leadership (Donnelly, 2020) is an important shift away from dualistic decision-making within Protestant congregational life.

Donnelly (2020) defined integrative polarity work as the ability to "navigate perceived oppositions and polarities both personally and collectively, so as not to fall into a simplistic either/other approach (p. 498). Younger clergy are becoming increasingly adept at this form of conflict mediation thanks to more varied professional backgrounds, expanded seminary training, and shifting worldviews of younger generations of Protestant pastors (Rohrer, 2020). This more expansive approach to problem-solving is especially important within Protestant church culture, where previous patterns of decision-making are deteriorating without new approaches firmly established.

While younger clergy are entering the ministry well-versed in adaptive leadership approaches, industrial CEO-style models of leadership continue pervade within "inherited churches" (Rohrer, 2020, p. 28). Rohrer described inherited churches as having deeply intrenched "institutional habits" that resemble capitalist business structures whereby the pastor is seen as a CEO hired to satisfy shareholder interests within the congregation. As Rohrer observed, "In that schema, we end up with a church that is for the smallest possible constituency, a pastor who cannot possibly please everyone, and an external, broader church and world that are not considered or engaged at all" (p. 28). Rohrer noted that this outcome-based, hierarchical model of leadership is grounded in male-centered individualistic leadership practices, which reinforce the notion of "mainline masculinity" within American Protestantism (Bendroth, 2022, p. 98). These established structures can create hostile work environments for younger clergy women who exhibit more inclusive and collaborative leadership approaches that promote shared power and decentralized leadership.

Hidden Dynamics

Due to the longer history and more widespread acceptance of women clergy within mainline American Protestantism, clergy women have the ability to push back against certain gendered expectations in ways that previous generations of women clergy could not (Zikmund et al., 1998). However, an ongoing challenge amid the increased autonomy and self-advocacy among today's Protestant clergy women is that there is no legal recourse for pastors whose intentional boundary-setting practices are rejected by parishioners. Due to church-state separation, ecclesial leaders, including Protestant clergy, are not afforded protection by anti-discrimination laws included in the United States' Title VII of the Civil Rights Act of 1964 and England's Equality Act of 2021 (Greene & Robbins, 2015, p. 406). This "ministerial exemption" is based on the ecclesial status of ordained clergy, who are generally considered outside of the bounds of secular legal protection (The Pew Forum, 2011).

With no legal oversight against such abuses as sexual misconduct, harassment, and unsafe work environments, today's women clergy find themselves in a precarious and vulnerable leadership space. When congregational conflict escalates, it is addressed, if at all, through internal denominational judicatory processes. The lack of secular legal involvement, coupled with ineffective denominational advocacy channels, poor accountability within local congregations, as well as the vocational commitment that certain women clergy maintain amid such challenges, results in a dangerous dynamic whereby individual women clergy can be systematically silenced, psychologically abused, and traumatized by their experiences in parish ministry.

Page and McPhillips (2021) highlighted the ways in which church-state separation has enabled religious institutions to avoid the secular judicial system. As "semi-independent bodies," church culture has been able to avoid certain financial and legal responsibilities, although that has come under heightened scrutiny due to increased prosecution of abuses of the Catholic Church and non-denominational religious sects in the United States and Australia (p. 156). Page and McPhillips pointed out that the sacralization of the priesthood, particularly male religious leadership, serves to protect male religious leaders and perpetuate systemic abuse against women and children in more insulated religious communities. While such gender-based violence is more overt within socially conservative faith communities, gender-based harassment and psychological abuse of younger clergy women has been systematically concealed within American Protestantism, where women's ordination is more generally accepted.

Jagger's (2021) work on symbolic violence in the Church of English offered important foundational work in addressing the often obscured and unrecognized violence perpetuated against women in roles of religious leadership. Jagger argued:

> Internalized religious discourses that establish divinely appointed complementary gender characteristics, arranged hierarchically, produce conditions in which gendered violence can occur in hidden ways. . . . Put simply, at the symbolic level, interactions that rob women of subjectivity and agency—discursively or materially—is symbolic violence. (p. 4)

Jagger applied Bourdieu's (1991) framework of symbolic violence to illustrate that interpersonal domination is expressed through everyday language in ways that can appear as relational, supportive, and collegiate yet, in reality, "humiliate, silence, isolate, and control" (Jagger, 2021, p. 7). Symbolic violence may be reflected in persistent comments on a woman pastor's physical appearance and/or sexuality, resistance to the appropriate use of maternity leave policies, judgement against women clergy who express emotion or demonstrate assertive leadership, and resentment toward women clergy who exhibit healthy boundaries around their pastoral role. While these exchanges may appear to be relatively civil encounters, beneath the surface are highly destructive disciplinary tools of shame and guilt (p. 5).

Symbolic violence is poorly recognized in ecclesial and domestic settings, due to their highly insular nature, which often prevents meaningful interventions. In order to make transparent the more hidden realities of psychological abuse against ordained women clergy, Jagger applied the Deluth Wheel of Power and Control (Pence & McDonnell, 1984). This diagnostic tool is a commonly used model by advocates of domestic abuse prevention as it identifies behavioral categories that constitute a violent relationship including intimidation, isolation, minimizing, blaming, and other forms of emotional and economic abuse. If one considers the often hidden and familial nature of Protestant church culture, coupled with ineffective accountability structures within local and denominational governance, there are striking parallels between the cycles of abuse within intimate partner relationships and the toxic dynamics of dysfunctional congregational systems.

3

PHILOSOPHICAL PILLARS

FEMINIST STANDPOINT AND GENDER-CRITICAL RESEARCH

As a feminist researcher, I understand gender identities, roles, and hierarchies to be socially constructed in ways that can harm, limit, and devalue individuals and groups. This feminist outlook informs my work as a leadership theorist, as I promote the foundational feminist position that the personal is political (Hanisch, 1970). This worldview extends to the ways in which I conduct research as well as interpret others' research in both religious and non-religious contexts. As a feminist epistemologist, I seek to highlight the sociology of knowledge production and engage in scholarship that resists sexist or androcentric research methods and interpretations (Longino, 2017). In doing so, I acknowledge the ways in which engrained gender narratives continue to restrict and oppress individuals and groups in their daily public and private lives.

My choice of constructivist grounded theory methodology for this study reflects this feminist critical outlook as "grounded theory has the potential to uncover the elusive qualities of the workplace, take the researcher beyond hegemonic understandings of organizations, and hold as central the participants and their stories" (Holloway & Schwartz, 2018, p. 497). Through my deliberate study design (Horan, 2024) and the interpretive lenses I used to analyze the research findings, I sought to prioritize the voices and meaning-making processes of the research participants and promote knowledge advancement that is human-centered, egalitarian, and liberative (Kushner & Marrow, 2003).

Through this feminist standpoint I recognize the ongoing struggle for gender equality, particularly with regard to the lived experiences of women and the multiple points of identity that interact with and intensify gender-based oppression. In order to deconstruct certain elements of feminism that reflect White privilege and heteronormativity, I applied the pluralistic approach of anti-racist feminisms (Liu, 2020, p. 104). In addition, I value womanist scholarship and its integration of gender and race criticism with liberative theological and spiritual frameworks, which offers an expansive approach to gender criticism and rejects essentialist understandings of gender and racial identities (Lightsey, 2015). Such intersectional approaches problematize what Schulz et al. (2018) described as WEIRD (Western, educated, industrialized, rich, and democratic) orientations to social theory, which need to be continually addressed if feminist theory is to effectively promote de-colonizing frameworks of social change. I applied these nonessentialist and intersectional commitments as I designed and conducted this study on the lived experiences of Protestant women clergy.

Advancements in gender equity and access to positions of leadership, particularly in the Global North during the past century, have caused some to take on a post-feminist view, which assumes that certain sectors of society have overcome gender-based oppression (Nast, 1992). Others maintain a "gender-conscious" view in which leaders are seen as significantly different and should be treated accordingly based on their gender identity, while others promote a "gender-blind" view that disregards any distinctions between gender (Jonsen et al., 2010, p. 556). This study on the psychological safety of Gen-X/Millennial clergy women reflects a third paradigm of "perception-creates-reality," in which leaders are not significantly different based on gender, however people believe they are different and these stereotypes create barriers to women's advancement.

EMBODIED LEADERSHIP AND PERCEPTION

Protestant church culture involves tacit and insidious elements of gender bias and conflicting gender-identity narratives, compared to the overt and denominationally sanctioned sexism of more theologically conservative religious traditions. In order to assess these more veiled expressions of gender discrimination, it is helpful to explore these issues through the lens of embodied leadership and perception. Embodied leadership is an emerging field of study that accounts for the interactions between sensing and perceiving bodies in the context of leadership. This field of research is rooted in the phenomenology of embodied perception put forth by French philosopher Maurice Merleau-Ponty (1945) and the lesser known yet seminal work of Simone Weil (1959).

Merleau-Ponty (1945) asserted that our understandings of human relationships are primarily based on our perceptions of one another, and those perceptions are rooted in our embodied experiences rather than at a strictly cognitive or rational level. The inner workings of human perception involve subconscious and pre-reflective processes that are deeply grounded in our somatic and sensory existence (Ladkin, 2012, p. 3). Merleau-Ponty's understanding of embodied perception moved beyond a merely sensorimotor level and provided the basis for understanding the ways in which we perceive and negotiate interpersonal boundaries (Leder, 1990).

While Merleau-Ponty's work is widely recognized as the primary backdrop for embodied leadership scholarship, it was another French philosopher, Simone Weil, who first elaborated on embodied perception a decade earlier. Weil (1959) pointed to the delicate nature of human boundaries through her understanding of friendship as a perilous balance between one's desire to consume and possess another, yet having the restraint to "look but not eat." Weil stated,

"[Friendship] is a miracle by which a person consents to view from a certain distance, and without coming any nearer, the very being who is necessary to him as food" (p. 35). This observation reflects the intimate nature of pastor-parishioner relationships in which parishioners exhibit varying degrees of restraint when it comes to respecting the pastoral boundaries of younger women clergy.

In her work on embodied leadership, Ladkin (2012) assessed the critical role that embodied perception plays in leader-follower relations, which has strong applicability to the experiences of women clergy in American Protestantism. Ladkin argued that the relational space between leader and follower is driven by perceptions, which "cannot occur without bodies to perceive and to be perceived" (p. 2). The way a follower "feels" about a leader is based on one's own social location and embodied experience. This process is often spoken about in terms of a "'gut feel' reaction and sensory response" and is the basis for our initial judgements about others, which is particularly important in determining a leader's trustworthiness (p. 2). The liminal space and often-subconscious nature of embodied perception is where leader and follower relations are most readily enacted, with potentially damaging consequences for the interpersonal boundaries and psychological safety of women leaders.

There is a precarious aspect to embodied perception that occurs when there is incongruence between the impression a leader intends to give and the resulting perception of the follower. The discrepancy can determine whether one's leadership is considered by others as effective, meaningful, and appropriate versus ineffective and passive, or aggressive and threatening. Ladkin (2008) observed this disconnect between the impression that a leader "gives," which the leader is in control of, and the impression that a leader "gives off," which the viewer or follower interprets and is in control of (p. 38). The work of impression management is a critical leadership practice, particularly for younger clergy women, where conflicting gender identity narratives create a striking disconnect between pastor-parishioner perceptions.

Gender and Embodied Leadership

The field of embodied leadership provides significant insight into the subconscious ways in which leader-follower relations are enacted. However, only recently have these discussions included the role of gender and the experience of women leaders within traditionally male-centered leadership contexts. O'Neill (2018) argued that women's bodies in spaces of leadership are not afforded the same sense of neutrality and are instead highly scrutinized. The historical normativity of masculine leadership "bestows upon the male body the advantage of invisibility" (p. 297). Lewis and Simpson (2010) observed that the "disembodied normatively" of the male body in leadership is precisely what allows the male body to go "unnoticed" (p. 5) and more readily accepted. Such heightened visibility of women leaders, reveals continued gender inequality and interpersonal power dynamics that severely compromise the psychological safety and leadership efficacy of younger clergy women.

During the early 2000s, the term "authentic leadership" began to take root, as leadership scholars explored how gendered expectations influence the development of trust and confidence in leader-follower relationships. Grounded in positive psychology, authentic leadership theories share two fundamental tenets: the concept of a 'true self' and a connection with ethics and morality (Gardner et al., 2011). Liu et al. (2015) built on these tenets, arguing that authentic leadership "depends on the leader performing authenticity in line with gender norms deemed appropriate for the socially constructed context in which they are expected to lead" (p. 237).

There has been an important shift within leadership scholarship whereby authenticity is no longer seen as attributional, in which leaders have certain internal capabilities that allow them to "do" authenticity. Instead, perceptions of a leader's authenticity are highly implicated in the leader's gender role performance and conformity to surrounding gender narratives (Lawler & Ashman, 2012; Sinclair, 2013). By challenging the gender neutrality of authentic leadership, emerging scholarship on embodied leadership has been able to pay particular attention to the ways in which gender expectations are constructed and perpetuated, which has strong application to the gendered expectations and leadership boundaries of younger women clergy.

Research on clergy women through the lens of embodied leadership has been more prominent in England and Australia where women's ordination is more recent and gender discrimination is more overt (Roberts, 2016). Within American Protestantism, where women's ordination is more firmly established, research has focused more on recommended coping strategies for the daily stresses of ordained ministry (Zikmund et al., 1998), instead of addressing underlying social system dynamics and negative perceptions towards women clergy. The study presented here is the first application of embodied leadership theory to explore the unique brand of antagonism faced by younger clergy women with strong boundary-setting practices within mainline American Protestantism.

LEADERSHIP BOUNDARIES AND PSYCHOLOGICAL SAFETY

What causes certain individuals to respect clergy women boundaries while others outwardly reject them? Whose boundaries do we see as valid or invalid and who gets to decide? How are leaders' interpersonal and professional boundaries enacted, how are they perceived by others, and what role does gender play?

Interpersonal Boundaries and Self-Differentiation

Due to the high boundary permeability of congregational life, clergy must be highly skilled in maintaining their own self-differentiation, in which one is conscious of the delicate balance between separateness and connection in relations to others. Self-differentiation involves identification with another's emotional state, yet at the same time maintaining one's own separate and distinct self. Cataldi (1993) described this relational space as "lived distance" that both unites and separates, in which one consciously observes "a place in which I am not" (p. 45). In her work on relational teaching, Schwartz (2019) described this process of self-differentiation as a "conscious and ever-evolving sense of where our experience and emotion stops and where [another's] starts" (p. 21).

Within Protestant church culture, zones of authority are highly flexible and blurred, due to the familial nature of congregational culture as well as reduced clerical authority. Within this context, maintaining healthy boundaries involves deep self-awareness and continual assessment of relational dynamics. This interior work is essential as it enables individual leaders to recognize others' boundaries while also observing one's own internal cues and re-establish equilibrium after boundaries have been pushed or compromised (Faraj and Yan, p. 607). It is this uncertain terrain that clergy women must constantly negotiate, particularly within congregations with conflicting gender narratives and intense levels of emotional projection that can compromise one's psychological safety.

Women Leaders and Psychological Safety

Workplace psychological safety refers to the feeling that one can be one's authentic self among others, with a sense of freedom to interact without compromising one's own identity. Psychological safety allows employees "to feel safe at work in order to grow, learn, contribute, and perform effectively" in a demanding role (Edmondson & Lei, 2014, p. 23). In addition, psychological safety enables an individual sense of trust, security, and relationship-building capacity within high stakes work environments (Edmondson & Lei, 2014).

Gender and leadership scholars have explored the psychological safety of individual women leaders, drawing on a larger body of research on gender bias as it relates to women in executive leadership positions. In historically male-centered leadership spaces, the perceived incompatibility between women's cis-gender identities and executive leadership roles (Eagly & Karau, 2002) has resulted in increased scrutiny and criticism of women executives compared to male executive leaders (Gupta et al., 2018). Dwivedi et al. (2023) revealed that women leaders are "chronically" and "acutely aware" of these disadvantages and, as a result, experience a sense of psychological threat within their leadership contexts (p. 1262). Women leaders who have felt their psychological safety is compromised, described the feeling as a lack of belonging and a heightened perception of threat and interpersonal risk, resulting in "push-to-leave" forces that motivated their decisions to leave toxic work environments (Dwivedi et al., 2023, p. 1263).

Another element of psychological safety for women leaders is the "glass cliff" phenomenon (Ryan & Haslam, 2005), which highlights the potential for women leaders to be placed in precarious leadership positions due to gendered assumptions of female relationality. However, when the same woman leader emphasizes task-oriented and agentic leadership skills, often required within high conflict contexts, such perceived masculinized traits set the woman leader apart from other women in the organization. By exhibiting gender-role incongruency, such women leaders are perceived by other women as undermining female group identity narratives, a phenomenon referred to as the "queen bee effect" (Ellemers et al., 2012, p. 183). Women executive leaders are often extremely aware of the conflicting gender-identity narratives they must negotiate on a moment-by-moment basis, which continually compromises their psychological safety.

Despite the expanded presence of women at all levels of denominational leadership, and the growing proportion of women seminarians and ordained clergy, there continues to exist local congregational beliefs, perceptions, and practices that question, resist, and ultimately reject certain expressions of women's pastoral authority (Campbell-Reed, 2019), leading to a violations of clergy women boundaries and threats to their psychological safety.

Beneath the Burnout

Research on gender, psychological safety, and leadership boundaries have, in some cases, reinforced harmful gender narratives, particularly around discussions on professional burnout. Those who study compassion fatigue and emotional burnout among women leaders often recommend that women leaders develop more rigorous self-care and coping strategies (Frame, 2004; Greene & Robbins, 2015; Myers, 2020). These observations have been made within caregiving professions including pastoral ministry (Greene & Robbins, 2015, Page, 2016), clinical therapy (Burke, 2022), and collegiate student affairs (McKinney, 2022).

Such research takes a personal responsibility stance toward boundary regulation and psychological safety, placing the onus on individual women leaders to establish more effective coping mechanisms that manage professional stress, such as individualized mentorship, counseling, or therapy. In addition, research on the work-family interface and work-life balance (Ammons, 2013; Frame, 2004; Glavin et al., 2011; McKinney, 2022; Polka et al., 2008) has the tendency to essentialize women as soft on boundaries and therefore more prone to stress, guilt, and overwhelm. Such research calls upon individual women to overcome their own unique workplace challenges, rather than critiquing the overarching gendered construction of leadership boundaries and behavioral practices that question women's boundary setting (Becker, 2020).

In light of these oversimplified solutions, feminist and constructivist research has begun to unpack the larger systems of oppression that reject the boundary-setting practices of women leaders (Becker, 2020; Diehl & Dzubinski, 2016; Marrone et al., 2018; Ryan & Haslam, 2005, 2007). Such research reveals a catch-22 dynamic in which women who allow more porous boundaries are valued, due to traditional gender-role congruency (Eagly & Karau, 2002), yet such boundary permeability ultimately leads to emotional and professional burnout. On the other hand, women leaders who maintain healthy interpersonal boundaries are often ridiculed for being too rigid, assertive, or aggressive (Marrone et al., 2018). This double-bind expectation is highly reflective of the experiences of Gen-X/Millennial clergy women whose boundary-setting practices are rejected in ways that severely compromise their individual psychological safety.

In their work on gender and burnout, Nagoski and Nagoski (2020) referred to societal expectations of the self-sacrificial and boundaryless woman as the "human giver syndrome," whereby women are expected to "give to humanity through their time, attention, affection, and bodies" (p. xiii). Human givers who attempt to care for themselves through certain self-protective boundaries face punitive measures in both private and public spheres where women's interpersonal boundaries are rejected. Moreover, there is continued cultural grooming within White, Western, and economically privileged social contexts for women to be perfectionists, overachievers, and people pleasers, which often aids in women securing high-level leadership positions. However, these are the very qualities that cause women to hold less stringent boundaries and experience emotional and physical burnout in those same leadership roles (Nagoski & Nagoski, 2020).

In order to account for the limitations in prior research on the psychological safety of women leaders, this study was attentive to the ways in which clergy women expressed self-differentiation and the resulting pushback and rejection of their healthy interpersonal boundaries. The research findings revealed a culture of feminized servanthood and systemic scapegoating, in which Gen-X/Millennial clergy women must negotiate contradicting gender expectations of their performance as a pastor, a leader, and a woman, in ways that are dehumanizing and abusive.

PART II

FINDINGS

4

THE SHADOW SIDE OF SERVANT-LEADERSHIP

During the winter and spring of 2024, I interviewed 20 Protestant clergy women, who represent a growing community of female pastors who have left a specific position or overall active ministry due to violations of their interpersonal boundaries and threats to their psychological safety. Despite the over 50 respondents, the research methodology and study design I chose utilizes a smaller population sample in order to more closely examine the social dynamics at play (Charmaz, 2003, Horan, 2024). To protect anonymity, each of the women's names have been changed in the following discussion and interview excerpts.

Throughout each stage of research, I sought to accurately reflect the layered experiences of the women participants, prioritizing their own meaning-making processes, thoughts, images, and language. The themes and categories outlined in the following chapters are drawn from the verbatim language used by the research participants, which enhances the agency within the women's lived experiences and reinforces the overall validity of the research findings. The six-month intensive process of data collection and analysis resulted in 280 pages of interview transcripts and 2,086 coded interview excerpts, which together convey a deep understanding of the underlying social dynamics within Protestant church culture.

Demographics

As illustrated in Figure 4.1, the research participants represented eight different mainline Protestant denominations, covering geographic areas predominantly in the Midwest, Pacific Northwest, Northeast, South, and Southeast, as well as two participants ordained within American denominations but pastoring churches in Canada and Europe. Ages ranged from 28–54, with the majority of participants being ages 41–47 and being on the cusp of Millennial and Gen X generations. Five women identify as LGBTQ+, with some noting that they had not fully disclosed their identities within their ministry contexts, which impacted their feelings of psychological safety and negotiation of certain gender role expectations. Marital status and family composition varied significantly, including participants who were married, divorced, partnered, or single, with balanced representation between those with no children, young children, or adult children.

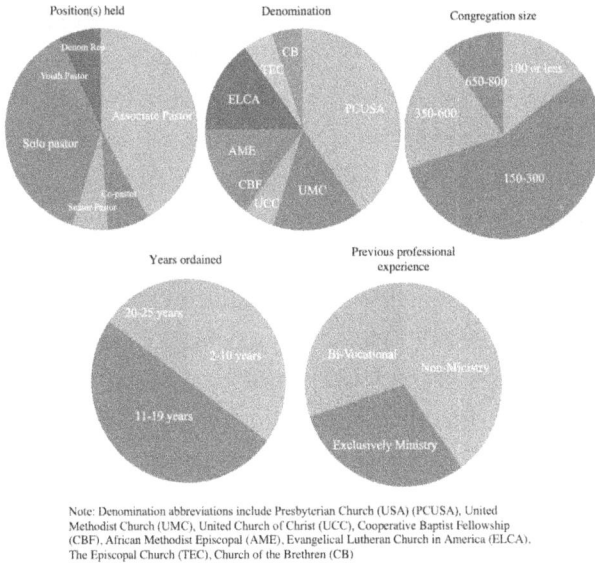

Note: Denomination abbreviations include Presbyterian Church (USA) (PCUSA), United
Methodist Church (UMC), United Church of Christ (UCC), Cooperative Baptist Fellowship
(CBF), African Methodist Episcopal (AME), Evangelical Lutheran Church in America (ELCA),
The Episcopal Church (TEC), Church of the Brethren (CB)

Figure 4.1: Aggregate Professional Demographic Data

Throughout this study I sought to recruit a racially diverse group of research participants, including Black, Latina, and Asian-American clergy women, with the understanding that racial marginalization exists within American Protestant church culture in distinct ways (Mosley-Monts, 2022). As a race-critical researcher committed to anti-racist feminisms, I applied intentional recruitment strategies to engage racially diverse perspectives. Despite these efforts, the majority of the research participants are White and worked in historically White denominations, and two women are Black and worked in historically Black denominations. This disparity is likely due to the long-term effects of racial segregation within American Protestantism, the resulting development of distinct clergy networking groups, as well as my own identity as a White researcher from a predominantly White religious tradition. Based on this limitation, there is a need for further research that explores the intersecting layers of marginaliza-tion and overlapping systems of gender and racial oppression that effect today's clergy women.

The clergy women in this study had a broad range of professional experiences prior to ordained ministry, which highlighted participants' exposure to different social dynamics, behaviors, and employment policies with which to compare their pastoral leadership experiences. Eight of the participants had non-ministry professions prior to entering ordained ministry, including the fields of art, law enforcement, human resources, and business management, among others. Of the remaining 12 participants, six participants had exclusively ministerial experience, including those who directly entered pastoral leadership as well as those who worked in chaplaincy, youth ministry, and retreat center administration. The remaining six participants who had prior ministry experience identified as being bi-vocational, having maintained part-time ministry work while also holding non-ministry positions often in the non-profit, social services, or education sectors. This range of professional experience proved to be significant as it alerted many of the participants to behaviors and social dynamics that were not experienced or tolerated in other professional contexts.

Research Findings: What All is Involved Here?

The purpose behind this research was to explore the lived experiences of younger clergy women and their decisions to leave active ministry, honor their perspectives, engage their own unique thoughts and language, and present the overarching relational dynamics as accurately and detailed as possible. Through the complex process of comparing and analyzing the interviews, themes or dimensions began to emerge that shed light on "What *all* is involved here?" (Schatzman, 1991). As Table 4.1 illustrates, the coded interviews began to take shape revealing core and primary dimensions, conceptual categories, and corresponding social processes, which served to develop concrete social and relational theory.

Through a rigorous qualitative research process known as dimensional analysis, two core dimensions or categories emerged from the compiled interviews: 1) *experiencing feminized servanthood as dehumanizing* and 2) *experiencing feminized servanthood as abusive*. These co-core dimensions "energize and connect the other dimensions but are also dependent on and interact with each other" (Schwartz and Holloway, 2017, p.42). Extending from these overarching elements were five additional dimensions: 1) *developing a sense of call;* 2) *differentiating self from system;* 3) *exposing vs. protecting toxic leaders and harmful systems;* 4) *nail in the coffin;* and 5) *reconstituting self* (see Table 4.1).

Co-Core Dimensions	Conceptual Categories and Corresponding Social Processes			
Experiencing feminized servanthood as dehumanizing	**Embodying the self-sacrificial woman** • People-pleasing, overfunctioning • Twisting myself into knots • Harmful humility	**Being invisibilized** • Not taking up space • Restricting voice, agency and authority • Shutting down opinions and ideas	**Absorbing others' emotions** • Holding others' discomfort • Shutting off my emotions • Being softest version of myself
Experiencing feminized servanthood as abusive	**Soul being chipped away (Psychological)** • Shocking and freezing • Feeling ripped to shreds • Punching bag for others' emotions	**Feeling decimated (Physical)** • Others needing to possess or control my body • No longer functioning • Just one death threat	**Naming the abuse and trauma** • Mirroring domestic violence • Love bombing and narcissistic abuse • Spiritual abuse
Primary Dimensions			
Developing a sense of call (Entering the system)	**Prepared and not prepared** • Not naïve coming in • Reluctant entry	**Finding myself in seminary** • Embracing a language of justice	**Losing myself in seminary** • Doors closing
Differentiating self from system	**Decentralizing leadership** • Equipping others and sharing power • Bringing people to the table • Meeting people where they are	**Conflicting gender narratives** • Gendered infantilizing • Mother-daughter wound • Disrupting masculinity	**Negotiating expectations & boundaries** • Porous boundaries • Buffering bullshit • Unspoken and double-bind expectations
Exposing and protecting toxic leaders and harmful systems	**Dealing with toxic leaders** • Toxic masculinity, throwing weight around • Internalized sexism • Others controlling/manipulating the narrative	**Your voice has no reality** • Gaslighting • Vortex of insanity • Thrown under the bus	**No one taking a stand** • Fed to the wolves • Dismissing sexual misconduct • Moral disalignment
Nail in the coffin	**Becoming the target** • Lightening rod • Scapegoating • Ousting the threat	**Life was threatened** • Not seen as human • Body taking me out • Staying will kill you	**Deciding to leave** • Vulnerability in betrayal • Throwing my hands up • Saving my life
Reconstituting self (Leaving the system)	**Metabolizing feelings** • Finding truth in emotions • Recovering from trauma • Letting go of guilt and shame	**Embodying uncertainty** • Questioning self and identity • Is the church good? • Healing takes time	**Remembering who I am** • Unlearning conditioned responses • Tending to what I want • Saving and liberating self

Copyright 2024 by Lynn M. Horan

Table 4.1: Explanatory Matrix

It is important to note that while the above table appears somewhat chronological, following each participants' journey in, through, and beyond their harmful ministry contexts, the reflections shared in each interview were often non-linear due to highly complex interactions, memories, experiences of trauma, and self-realizations that were shared by the participants. This more "navigational stance" (Roberts, 2022, p. 102) is observed throughout the following chapters, which offer concept-by-concept analysis of the explanatory matrix illustrated above. Noted in italics, each category and its component social processes are drawn directly from the concrete patterns and themes described by the participants. Woven between the verbatim interview excerpts is relevant social theory used to develop new understandings of these often-silenced realities within Protestant church culture.

FEMINIZED SERVANTHOOD AS DEHUMANIZING AND ABUSIVE

The overarching social process that was described by the clergy women participants was the experience of feminized servanthood as being both dehumanizing and abusive. The participants' experiences reflected highly gendered understandings of serving others, which included both implicit and explicit messages from others within church and denominational systems. In addition, the women described social conditioning and internalized messages of female servanthood from within their own self-understanding, families of origin, and overall faith journey. These gendered understandings of servitude impacted the women's experiences of psychological abuse by the surrounding church culture, both for those clergy women who internalized gendered expectations of self-sacrifice as well as those who resisted or questioned the gender narrative of the self-sacrificial woman. The participants' experiences of feminized servanthood as both dehumanizing and abusive is outlined in detail below, utilizing the participants' own verbatim language categories (see Figure 4.2).

Co-Core Dimensions

DEHUMANIZING		ABUSIVE
• Embodying the self-sacrificial woman	**Experiencing feminized servanthood as**	• Soul being chipped away
• Being invizibilized		• Feeling decimated
• Absorbing others' emotions		• Naming abuse and trauma

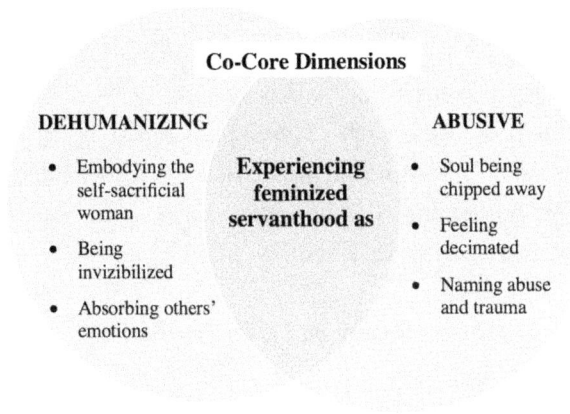

Figure 4.2: Co-Core Dimensions and Corresponding Conceptual Categories

Feminized Servanthood as Dehumanizing

Following the opening interview question, "What has been your experience as a clergy woman?", the participants described in detail various gendered expectations around their pastoral role, as well as reactivity from others when they did not demonstrate or reflect implicit or explicit gendered norms. Based on this consistent sharing, the central category of *experiencing feminized servanthood as dehumanizing* emerged. As outlined in Table 4.2, the clergy women described how both internal and external expectations of *embodying the self-sacrificial woman, being invisibilized,* and *absorbing others' emotions,* strongly informed their experiences as pastoral leaders.

First Co-Core Dimension	Conceptual Categories and Corresponding Social Processes		
Experiencing Feminized Servanthood as Dehumanizing	**Embodying the Self-Sacrificial Woman** • People-pleasing and over-functioning • Twisting myself into knots • Harmful humility	**Being Invisibilized** • Not taking up space • Restricting voice, agency and authority • Shutting down opinions and ideas	**Absorbing Others' Emotions** • Holding others' discomfort • Shutting off my emotions • Being softest version of myself

Table 4.2: First Co-Core Dimension: Experiencing Feminized Servanthood as Dehumanizing

Embodying the Self-Sacrificial Woman

The category of *embodying the self-sacrificial woman* involved three primary social processes, each of which included both internal and external messages. These social processes were identified as: *people-pleasing and over-functioning, twisting myself into knots*, and *harmful humility*, which will be described in detail below.

People-pleasing and Over-functioning

An important part of the category of *embodying the self-sacrificial woman* was the interplay between 1) external expectations placed upon the women within their ministry contexts and 2) internalized messages and conditioning that the women absorbed from their families of origin, community, and/or religious upbringing. Rose shared an important observation of people-pleasing that developed during her childhood and later fed into expectations of her pastoral role:

> Growing up I didn't have a great self-esteem. I didn't have a great sense of self love. So, I was always pouring out from an empty space within myself and giving whatever I had to someone else because then I had something to tap into that gave me value. I was always just pushing people forward behind the scenes but not realizing that I was letting go pieces of myself as I was people-pleasing.

Sarah described entering ordained ministry wanting to fulfill others' needs in order to validate her leadership as a woman. However, she felt this default approach ultimately compromised her ability to lead with integrity:

> I was such a people pleaser early in my ministry because I just wanted them to like me and think I was doing a good job. And I care that I do a good job and good ministry, but I feel less and less like that's for others to evaluate and more between me and

God of how I'm showing up and how I'm doing the work. And am I doing it with integrity? Or am I doing it just to be liked?

Several women recalled both internal and external messages that reinforced gendered expectations of the self-sacrificial woman as a helper or peace-maker. Melanie discussed the relational dynamic of co-dependency in which her internalized role of the helper reinforced others' expectations that she perform that role within her ministry context:

> I've worked hard on not letting people walk all over me. I was seeing a counselor and every time I told her a new story about a church member, she said, "I can't believe you have so many codependent people in your life." I think part of my own co-dependency comes from my family of origin, especially my mom. To this day, the most value that she sees in herself is how much she can help other people. If she's helping someone else, she has value. If other people like her, she has value. That was modeled pretty strong for me in my life.

Sandra noted how she felt her own over-functioning was both a necessity for the church's overall survival as well as a reflection of the church's preference for the male co-pastor, noting, "He kind of floated by and didn't do very much. The church wouldn't have functioned if I hadn't been there doing more. But he was the energetic face of the congregation and they really liked that." Jenny described her over-functioning as a kind of performance that others consumed, noting, "Nobody would come alongside and support the ministry and so I ended up burning myself out trying to do everything by myself with people just standing back sort of watching."

Over-functioning also came up consistently as a general job expectation, particularly for the women in associate pastor roles, where senior pastors (who were men in most but not all cases) would delegate an unrealistic amount of responsibilities. Vivienne described the idea of the "associate umbrella," which involved the ongoing tendency for senior pastors to off-load excessive responsibilities. This dynamic also included the gendered expectation of "cleaning up" or being the default person for various forms of damage control:

> It made me the bad guy in almost every scenario and people quickly came to dislike me. Not everyone, but it felt it was set up that way. He would wave to people and shake their hands and say "yes" and I'd come along and be like, "I'm sorry we do not have the budget for that" or "I'm sorry the building is already booked for that weekend." I was constantly apologizing and it almost became the stereotypical weird male and female roles because I was the woman apologizing behind him all of the time. It was a very bizarre setup. So, it was often the case that I was cleaning up after him. And I think emotionally some of the women who were being neglected on staff and then eventually shoved out had it very difficult and I, by default, became the person everyone called when it went south for them.

Rose observed a similar tendency for clergy women to be expected to "clean up" others' messes:

> I have often seen clergy women relegated to clean up a mess that a clergyman has created. We're always sent to fix it. We're always sent to rebuild it. Reshape it. Get the members back. You know, get ministries active again. And then as soon as that happens, we're moved. And we're moved to either fix once again another problem, another challenge.

Cora felt the gendered expectation of pleasing others and over-functioning was reinforced by other clergy and denominational leaders who conveyed the message of "winning them over":

> Of the four churches that I've served, there was always a contingent that I connected with and there was always a contingent that had really strong negative feelings. So that

was present everywhere I went. I was told that was "normal." That, if I was faithful, if I loved them, if I ignored the bad behavior then I would win them over. I just had to show them that, you know, having a young, single female pastor wasn't a bad thing. And if I did that, then, I would win them over. And of course, we know that occasionally that might happen with one or two people, but I don't think the system is set up for that.

Twisting Myself into Knots

The persistent expectations of people-pleasing and over-functioning operated both consciously and unconsciously and were informed by both internal and external messages. Over time, these gendered expectations began to wreak havoc on the women's physical and psychological well-being, which is reflected in the social process of *twisting myself into knots*. For some, like Miranda, the feeling of contorting oneself to fit others' expectations and fulfill others' needs was not so much an existential struggle as a frustration that wore on her, but to which she eventual became accustomed:

There's always this response to me and I am aware of it like this dance that I do inside. It's not even a struggle, it's just people initially always respond to me this way until they get used to me, until they get to know me and then it's okay. I want to be really generous with people, because a lot of the behavior will start to die down after a while. And then people get to know me and they're just like, "Oh! You DO know what you're talking about. Oh wow, you just saw me through a really hard time." It still feels kind of exceptional, like you're the exception, like we didn't like female priests, but you're the exception. Or we didn't like a gay priest, but you're the exception, the exceptional priest.

Haley, described similar experiences of receiving critical feedback, in which she felt like she needed to "twist myself into knots" in order to communicate effectively within a toxic ministry context:

> It was as if I am somehow defective because I cannot effectively communicate my ideas with these people. Communication is so much of what we do as pastors and it is a skill set that has to be learned and developed. You have to take feedback about whether or not it's effectively getting across to someone. I was always trying to take that feedback in and improve, but at some point my therapist said, "It's not that you can't clearly communicate your ideas. It's they just can't, they can't hear that." And I have gotten tired of twisting myself into knots to get someone to work with me as a leader when they don't want to.

Harmful Humility

As each of the women described both the psychological and physical impact of embodying the self-sacrificial woman in each of their ministry contexts, there were internal conversations that informed the women's experiences. The women would often recognize the unsustainability of certain expectations yet ultimately override those concerns with a strong sense calling or "sacrificial embrace" within their ministry contexts (Greene & Robbins, 2015). The minimizing, tolerating, and overriding that took place was often derived from unhealthy understandings and theologies of humility that the women had absorbed both within and beyond their ministry contexts, including expectations that were internal to their own self-understanding as well as explicitly communicated to them.

Deborah offered a powerful description of a particularly feminized form of faith-based service and what it felt like to "choose humility in an unhealthy way." In this description, she also foreshadowed certain life-threatening consequences that will be discussed further in the category of *feminized servanthood as abusive*:

In the denomination there's a really strong insistence that leaders are servant leaders. And so we have a real ambiguous understanding and relationship with power in any sense. And if you're a woman in leadership, that's doubled down on. If you're gonna play up here with the big players and you're a woman, then you better be humble about it, right? The women who have persevered and continued their careers in ministry are women who choose humility in an unhealthy way. And there's a huge cost to that. I've had three female colleagues who stayed in ministry long-term, each of whom have died of a ruptured brain aneurism.

Cora described her seminary education as contributing to unhealthy theologies of self-sacrifice and humility, which reinforced messages that she had received during her upbringing:

I remember in the first semester my professors telling me, "We are tearing down everything that you think you believe that you were taught growing up, to rebuild your theology." And I think what they didn't tell me but what I experienced, was that it also stripped me down personally. And so it kind of exacerbated things that I already had going on personally.

Jenny experienced similar theological underpinnings of unhealthy humility and the expectation to fit into a kind of "mold," which ultimately caused her to "lose herself" in the process:

In the church, I think I felt like I had to fit into some sort of mold. And if you don't think this way, then you're a heretic. When I was a full-time pastor, I felt like what the apostle Paul says, I was just "poured out like water." Just completely depleted. I heard stories about other pastors who were really supported by their congregation so that they could keep going and I felt like mine just kept trying to pull from me. In a time of prayer, the image I had of myself was in an ocean surrounded by the Holy Spirit in this bubble and fish and birds just trying to eat me. And that led to a lot of disappointment and a losing of myself.

Cindy described enduring suffering for the "sake of the call," which resulted in having to "take whatever people gave me" in ways that were deeply harmful psychologically:

The message I heard in seminary was people are gonna treat you poorly and it's just the thing you should expect. That's just part of what being a pastor means, that people are gonna project on you and they're going to say things to you that aren't about you. It's about what's going on with them and you need to find ways to process that. The expectation was that it was my responsibility to be self-contained emotionally and to deal with everything myself and to just sort of take whatever people gave me. And that being treated badly was sometimes just part of the calling. I would never have phrased it this way, but I did sort of feel like suffering for Jesus was kind of the thing I'm supposed to do and that kind of martyrdom thing that I was taught was honorable and was just part of being called. So that's what I should expect.

While some of the participants had strong internalized messages of harmful humility, there were others like Vivienne who did not profess a self-sacrificial theology, noting, "I do not profess a theology that requires me to suffer to become a better human. Yet I did experience darkness and felt isolated, often because it was such a difficult time." Like Vivienne, Joanna did not base her leadership on a strong sacrificial theology, yet her understanding of leadership maintained high levels of humility and self-sacrifice that manifested in intense anxiety and wishing "her body would cooperate":

During the panic attacks, my heart rate would just raise up and there was no stopping it from racing. I didn't have to go to an emergency room but it was just this overwhelming heart rate and emotional experience. I said to a friend, "If my body would just cooperate, I could stay at this church." And as soon as I said it, I heard what I said, I don't need you to repeat that back. I got it loud and clear. So, the embodied experience of suppressing your own needs is really, really damaging.

Being Invisibilized

Having outlined the category of *embodying the self-sacrificial woman,* the related category of *being invisibilized* involved a deeper layer of gendered self-sacrifice based on the women's own social conditioning to "not take up space," as well as others' overt efforts to contain, silence, restrict, and/or reject the voices and agency of the clergy women. The concept of *being invisibilized* points to both a spacial reality in which the women felt physically removed from decision-making spaces, as well as a relational reality in which their contributions were ignored, denied, or minimized. These social processes were described in the interviews as *not taking up space, restricting voice, agency and authority,* and *shutting down opinions and ideas.*

Not Taking Up Space

The process of *not taking up space* included both internalized messages that caused some women to try to "shrink themselves," as well as external messages from others within the ministry context to "not fully exist." As a solo pastor, Allegra noticed:

When I began to take up space, people didn't like that. Before it was "Allegra is just so nice and she just didn't get in our way. And we just loved that. And now she's making decisions that are uncomfortable for me and I have to actually deal with her as a human being."

Allegra also recalled being verbally attacked by a well-known male pastor at a denominational meeting, where she struggled between defending herself and surrendering to the power dynamics at play:

> I found myself standing my ground because I was trying to take up space because I've been trying to learn how to do that. In the same breath my body wanted to just run away. I did find myself saying, "Oh, ok, well, sorry you see it that way." But I'm so conditioned and if a male figure says something like this and gets in your face about it, then you need to back off and just don't make waves. Stop making waves.

Marta, an associate pastor, also used the language of not "taking up space," when reflecting on overt criticism of her ministry by male senior pastors she dealt with in each of the three different congregations where she worked. Marta noted:

> Instead of celebrating it and saying, golly, she's a phenomenal teacher, you should all go to her education class. Or look at this great pastoral care work that she's doing, let's encourage her to play to her strengths. Instead, I feel like from the heads of staff, it's just been how can we shut her down? How can we minimize her? Or let's not allow this woman to take up any of our space that we want to take up.

As a Black clergy woman working within an historically Black denomination, Rose's description of invisibilizing was informed by her understanding of misogynoir:

> I summarize misogynoir as a disdain for Black women and it goes a bit deeper than that. It misconstrues, misinterprets, misinforms people about the sacred text as it relates to women. Women tend to be unnamed. Women were caused harm through rape and abuse.
>
> Women are told to be silent. People interpret the Christian sacred text as women should not be pastors or leaders. So that

then spills out into this term misogynoir where it is very dehumanizing and oppressive. It invisibilizes Black women and Black women aren't treated equitably in the leadership of the denomination.

Restricting Voice, Agency, and Authority

Additional social processes were revealed whereby the women felt overt restriction of their ability to express themselves, make decisions, and assert pastoral authority that was well-within the purview of their positions as either associate pastors or senior pastors and heads of staff. Sandra described how transitions in pastoral leadership allowed her to see the stark contrast between working collaboratively with other leaders versus those who sought to silence and delegitimize her leadership:

> It was hostile. Quite openly hostile. On his first day on the job, people went to the new pastor and complained that I had just done this thing without them knowing or caring or understanding, even though it had been a project that had been spearheaded by the interim pastor that had left. And so the new pastor pulled me into his office within the first week of being there and reprimanded me for doing things that I wasn't allowed to do. From the very get-go, it was clear that he didn't trust me. He didn't ask me what happened. There was never a conversation. And so, I just kind of had to do my work in that uncertainty.

During Christy's first ordained position as an associate pastor, she was explicitly told by the female senior pastor, whose husband was a co-pastor with her, "You need to be subservient to us." This was shocking to Christy who had come from a family of pastors, both men and women. Christy also felt that when she shared specific knowledge that she had within a particular area of ministry, she felt that as a woman her assertiveness "came across as aggressive or rigid," which was perceived as threatening by the older female senior pastor. Christy later understood the senior pastor's reactivity as a need to control narratives within the church, which will be discussed further in the category of *exposing vs. protecting toxic leaders and harmful systems.*

The resistance toward voice, agency, and authority of each clergy woman came from multiple directions, including senior pastors, other church staff, and parishioners, regardless of gender. Joanna, a senior pastor and head of staff, expressed to an older female office administrator that it was inappropriate to work on personal projects during her allotted office hours, to which the woman "practically yelled at me saying 'I am not pausing on this!'" This confrontation ultimately set the stage for a larger staff-wide campaign to eliminate Joanna, which will be discussed further in the dimension of *becoming a target.* Further discussion on intergenerational conflict between women will be addressed in the category of *conflicting gender narratives.*

Vivienne, an associate pastor, described being "relieved of certain duties," which removed her as the only woman represented on important decision-making committees within the church. She felt this was an overt abuse of power that eliminated much-needed checks and balances to the senior pastor and those who surrounded him:

> I was relieved of some duties because I was saying that my workload was tremendous and that I wasn't getting enough off time with my family. The duties that I was relieved from were executive committee and HR, which are the two most important checks to the senior pastor's power. I was the only other female presence on staff and I was the only other pastor in those meetings. So, when the senior pastor relieved me of those duties there was no one else checking that power.

Shutting Down Opinions and Ideas

The women also experienced specific instances when their opinions or ideas were unwelcome, rejected, or only seen as valued when restated by another, usually male, pastor. Jenny, a senior pastor described the ways in which creative ideas were "smashed" and "shattered":

> When we had an associate pastor, he and I talked about not having the bandwidth to start anything new because pandemic ministry was exhausting. We were able to see how church could be done differently, bringing in new people who are totally uninterested in the worship service but could build community in other ways. But then that was just smashed up against a wall and just shattered into a thousand pieces.

Kay, also a solo pastor, saw an opportunity for her congregation to receive coaching from a denominational training program. When the denomination asked for volunteer churches and clergy to participate in the training, Kay felt her idea was silenced:

> I almost fell out of my chair and raised my hand so hard and I was like, "Pick us!" I was not trying to be a woman alone on an island fixing this church. I knew we needed help. I knew there were dynamics at this church that I wasn't entirely picking up on. And we just needed some assistance. But I just felt like my voice wasn't being heard.

Melanie, a senior pastor who had followed a very dis-engaged male pastor, shared that church members were consistently surprised or frustrated that she had an opinion, particularly among older women who felt a sense of pride and ownership within certain ministry areas:

> There was an older woman and then somebody that was close with her, who I think were surprised that I had any opinions about anything when I came back from maternity leave. I went to meetings and I was like, "Here's what we can do as a church," and they answered "Well no, you're not letting us run it our way. Why do you have an opinion on anything?"

Hope wasn't surprised by some of the silencing she experienced, particularly in the southern context where she lived and worked. She recognized the dynamic as something that wasn't going to change:

> I noticed right away some of the things you had to do. But this was in any workplace where when you're working with a male superior, you will bring up ideas and you get told they're not that great. And then two weeks later, they come into a meeting and they suddenly have this great idea that was your idea and you just go with it and you just kind of go, "Okay, whatever, as long as it's getting done, doesn't matter whose idea it was, blah blah blah."

Absorbing Others' Emotions

The final category in the area of *feminized servanthood as dehumanizing*, was the experience of *absorbing others' emotions*, which reflected the women's increased concern over their emotional well-being and psychological safety. The women described the long-term impact of absorbing unhealthy emotional projection from others, as well as doing the emotional labor of navigating and deescalating highly charged relational spaces. The primary social processes that emerged from this category were *holding others' discomfort, shutting off my emotions,* and *being the softest version of myself,* which severely compromised the women's overall physical and psychological well-being.

Holding Others' Discomfort

The language of "absorbing others emotional labor" first emerged with Haley who described what it felt like to "perform femininity" through "agreeableness" and "smoothing things over":

> Part of it is a kind of agreeableness and endless energy for holding other people's social shit and smoothing things over and just taking on all the responsibility for the emotional labor

in relationships when people weren't willing to do that. And that happened a lot, particularly with older men who just expected the woman in the room to make nice. My older clergy woman supervisor put the emotional labor on me of keeping that relationship running smoothly, when she was just actively trying to antagonize me.

When asked to describe the idea of "emotional labor" further, Haley offered an important description of what it means to "hold others' discomfort" within the context of racial justice work:

One of my pastor colleagues, who is a young man of color, queer person, talks about centering People of Color and what that requires of White people in the congregation and spreading the discomfort around and making White people do some work too. And that made something go off in my brain because I hold so much of other people's discomfort and try and smooth it over.

Cindy also faced the expectation that she comfort others while they were actively mistreating her. When others felt she did not uphold that expectation, she was punished in the form of church members' silence or other church members' decisions to leave the congregation in protest:

There was an expectation that I would not just take it but that my response to that would be particularly gentle and soft and non-confrontational. And the expectation was almost that I should make people feel better about being terrible to me. Like it was my responsibility to make them feel good about that or make them feel like they're still good people in the midst of it, which I just think is utter bullshit. I didn't fully buy into that, but it clearly was the expectation. And whenever I didn't do that, whenever I didn't respond that way, I was very clearly punished for it.

Sarah also experienced the expectation to bear the emotional burden of conflict and crisis within her church community. However, in her case there was an additional physical burden due to the intensity surrounding a very real and imminent death threat against her by a church member, which will be addressed further in the category of *feeling decimated:*

> Nobody questioned, "Are you okay standing up front leading every week?" Instead, I got a panic button underneath the pulpit. There were times when I was like, I can't. I can't be upfront today. I had to ask for that. If I felt like I just couldn't lead from up front because it was too scary, I had to ask to not have to that week. It wasn't like, "What do we need to do to help support her in the midst of this crisis?" The entire church was in crisis, but I was bearing the emotional and physical burden of this.

Shutting Off My Emotions

The clergy women also described the need to shut off their own emotions in the midst of conflict or disagreement. Cindy felt it was particularly dehumanizing to not be able to express anger as a woman:

> There were many times when I was responding to something that church members actually were saying to me and having legitimate emotional responses to people saying very cruel things to me. And not feeling allowed to tell them that they needed to stop, or that it was an inappropriate thing to say. I especially shut off any feelings of anger and the ability to express that to people in my churches. What I've realized is that Christian culture really doesn't want women in particular to express anger at all.

In addition to external expectations, Jenny felt that suppressing her emotions was further intensified by her understanding of self-worth and the narrative of the "good girl":

> People would treat me badly and I made excuses for them. I had a habit of giving people the benefit of the doubt and excusing their behavior without recognizing how it affected me. I wonder if this is related to the narrative that I have to be a "good girl." In that sense, if something went wrong, it must mean that I wasn't good enough, that I have to pivot to be good enough to make things better. I need to comfort or support this person even though it's negatively affecting me.

Being the Softest Version of Myself

Cindy described the process of being the "softest version" of herself as she addressed her congregation's mis-treatment of a nonbinary staff member. Cindy carefully voiced her concerns with the congregation, which caused many to resent her for "shaming them":

> I was very careful to make sure to say it kindly and to try to be the softest version of myself as possible. I really worked at that. And yet people felt shamed by that and responded by just digging their heels in. Instead of addressing the problem they chose to just be angry at me for shaming them. And I couldn't recover from that. My impression of the congregation and my hope for church was shattered by that response and that's when I left.

Other women described the process of "accommodating others," which became psychologically damaging for those with previous experiences of PTSD. Jenny described the work of "accommodation" becoming unsustainable when it brought to the surface the pain and trauma she experienced after having had a stillbirth:

When the pandemic hit, for me all of the PTSD from the still-birth came back and I was living that again. I could feel it. And there was a minister who insisted on getting married at the church even though everything was shut down. I was still in the mode of accommodating people so I worked so hard to figure out what could be done. There was no compromising with them, no understanding that it just wasn't possible. I was also trying to figure out how to keep everyone connected, working seven days a week while the church board was just sitting at home. I couldn't handle it and I needed to go on a health leave but it was done in a very condescending way.

In the categories described above, each contributed to the overarching dimension of experiencing *feminized servanthood as dehumanizing*. The compounded effect of both internalized messages and external expectations of the self-sacrificial woman created an extremely restricted space of existence for each of the women, in which their agency and overall humanity was compromised. As these experiences escalated and intensified further, the women described the more acute and at times life-threatening realities of *feminized servanthood as abusive*.

Feminized Servanthood as Abusive

The ongoing experience of leading within these harmful conditions led to severe cases of psychological stress and abuse, which came under the umbrella of *experiencing feminized servanthood as abusive*. This dimension emerged more gradually throughout each interview, after the women had laid the framework for their *experiences of femininized servanthood as dehumanizing*. The women were able to endure certain elements of feminized servanthood while still exhibiting agency and important leadership choices, which will be further discussed in the category of *differentiating self from system*. However, as the clergy women moved further into their ministry experiences, social processes began to emerge that looked and felt like abuse, whether physical, emotional, or spiritual, even if the women were not able to articulate it at the time. The following discussion outlines the dimension of *experiencing feminized servanthood as abusive*, which is illustrated by the categories of *soul being chipped away (psychological)*, *feeling decimated (physical)*, and *naming the abuse and trauma*, along with their corresponding social processes (see Table 4.3).

Second Co-Core Dimension	Conceptual Categories and Corresponding Social Processes		
Experiencing Feminized Servanthood as Abusive	**Soul Being Chipped Away (psychological)** • Shocking and freezing • Feeling ripped to shreds • Punching bag for others' emotions	**Feeling Decimated (physical)** • Others needing to possess/control my body • No longer functioning • Just one death threat	**Naming the Abuse and Trauma** • Mirroring domestic violence • Love bombing and narcissistic abuse • Spiritual abuse

Table 4.3: Second Co-Core Dimension: Experiencing Feminized Servanthood as Abusive

Soul Being Chipped Away (psychological)

The categories of *soul being chipped away (psychological)* and *feeling decimated (physical)* include lengthy excerpts from a few key interviews, which incapsulate the intensity of the psychological and physical damage that each woman experienced. These incidents are not considered outliers, but are highly reflective of repeating patterns seen in each of the interviews and are supported by additional shorter excerpts.

Shocking and Freezing

Joanna, a solo pastor and head of staff, experienced an inappropriate physical encounter with a male congregant that illustrated the feeling of "freezing," in which she felt stunned, surprised, and unable to process the incident in the moment. Her psychological safety was further compromised by the subsequent minimizing of the experience both by her own internalized messages and social conditioning as well as normalizing of the behavior from other staff members. During the interview, she initially described the incident very briefly and without much detail:

Yeah, not overwhelming, but not anything I would want for anyone. And that concept of him scanning the room to realize he had this opportunity was, you know, chilling. I set it aside for a while mentally for a couple of weeks and then I realized there were still residual emotional effects of this.

When asked to describe what she felt in that moment, she noted the concept of "freezing" and her own internal thought process that caused her to minimize the experience:

He found an opportunity where I was in a secluded area and it just had that, that kind of, power play vibe to it. He found a way to invade my personal space, and I froze. I'm 47 and I don't feel like I was taught much about "freeze or fawn." I was taught "fight or flight," so that never made sense to me when I didn't say something or respond in a way that I usually would. It felt very invasive but part of me thought I was kind of beyond that. There were probably times in my ministry where similar kinds of touch had happened early on and I honestly just normalized it as just mild sexual harassment. But as a grown woman in ministry, I was not at all prepared to have that experience.

Joanna felt her psychological safety was further compromised by the personnel committee's dismissal of the incident, in which both men and other woman said, "You're welcome to press charges but it's not our responsibility." She felt "up against a wall" if she did anything due to the fact that the man was a prominent church member's son. Further discussion on the lack of support from other women leaders in the congregation is included in a later section on the social process of *conflicting gender narratives.*

Joanna's experience highlighted several notable themes seen in other interviews including 1) placing sole responsibility on the pastor to address concerns with the perpetrator; 2) the desire to protect prominent leaders and/or members of the congregation; and 3) church leadership showing interest in the pastor's safety only if framed as a safety issue for the larger congregation.

Feeling Ripped to Shreds

Marta, an associate pastor serving in a multi-staff church, had a male senior pastor whose approach to leadership included intense verbal and psychological abuse, which left her feeling "torn up" and "ripped to shreds." The lengthy excerpt included below represents consistent themes found in other interviews, including 1) economic insecurity and the need to maintain employment amid ongoing abuse; 2) criticism extending beyond immediate incidents and including broader accusations of the clergy woman's character, personality, and physical body; 3) additional forms of punishment including being assigned a mentor and being instructed to make amends with other individuals; 4) the need for therapy specifically for trauma recovery in order to reconstitute oneself after intense abuse; and 5) the realization that this was "not right," both during and especially after the traumatic event(s).

The following encounter took place in the senior pastor's office in the presence of six other female church members who were critical of Marta's engagement with a summer youth program:

I get into this horrible meeting and without the senior pastor saying it directly outright, I knew that whatever happened in this meeting was going to determine my employment at the church. It had been made that clear. At the beginning of the meeting, I was told I would not be allowed to speak. I had to listen to these six women, in turn, tear me up. Not just about the youth activity but about everything I had done since day one of my ministry that they did not like. They attacked my ministry. They attacked my character. And not only did he allow them to do that, he encouraged them, egging them on, saying, "Oh, well tell her, too, about how she dresses. You talked about that to me and she needs to hear that too."

In addition to the emotional impact, Marta's employment security was in the forefront of her mind and informed her response to the criticism:

> By the time it was my turn to speak, I had so much emotional shit basically put on me, I just burst into tears. And then what are you going to do, right? I was 33, single and dependent on this job for which I'm barely making ends meet. I can't get fired. You know, I'm applying for jobs, but I'm not there yet in terms of finding something. And so I had to go around to each of these women in turn and apologize. Sometimes genuinely apologize and sometimes just apologize to get through the meeting.
>
> And then one of the women, probably the nicest of the six, said, "You know, I know this meeting's been hard. So, I just want to tell you why I appreciate your ministry. And I just want to let you know that I forgive you." Then she looked at the other five women and the senior pastor to kind of be like, "Okay, now it's your turn. Like we've already torn her apart. Let's try to put some of this back together." And they all just stared at her.

The meeting left Marta feeling "ripped to shreds" with no ability to defend herself and ultimately being congratulated by the senior pastor for enduring the psychological abuse:

> And at the end of this meeting, after I'm still crying and have just been ripped to shreds for five years' worth of stuff, the senior pastor had the gall to look at me and say, "Marta would you please pray to close the meeting for us?" And I wanted to say no, but I felt like I could not say no.
>
> After the meeting finished, I was in my office, and the senior pastor literally stands in my doorway. Physically takes up all the space, so even if I wanted to leave, I couldn't get around him. And he's like, "You did a good job today. This could have gone

very differently. If it had gone very differently, this probably would have had a very different outcome." Really implying that apparently, I had done enough to keep my job.

Punching Bag for Others' Emotions

Marta's experience was mirrored by other women who described constant emotional abuse within their ministry contexts. Allegra described being "screamed at" on several occasions and ultimately feeling like a "punching bag for others' emotions." With prior training in family systems theory, Allegra did what she could to coach herself through some extremely difficult interactions:

> I remember a woman who got mad at me for asking to put a projector screen in the church. You'd have thought I was bringing the devil himself into church. She literally screamed at me. But that's not the first time I've ever been screamed at by a church member. While pastoring another church I got screamed at and cornered by a middle-aged woman who said that I wasn't doing things right. In looking back on it, I feel like maybe she was threatened by me or something, but it was a lot of screaming.
>
> Even though I know what's going on and I'm trying to have this conversation and almost coach myself through it, it still feels awful because you're like, why are you yelling at me? I'm still a human being. Why are you taking this out on me? Why? Why have I become this projection for your feelings about this? This hurts!
>
> I would go home sometimes crying because I was holding all this emotional baggage from people taking stuff out on me, you know. And I don't think you can function very well if you're constantly being a punching bag, if you're constantly the container for other people's emotional baggage, that they haven't worked through for themselves. And there is an expectation that I would just take it.

Others described similar feelings of being overwhelmed by the constant emotional projection of parishioners and other church leaders. Kay remembered "feeling toward the end I felt like I was drowning. It just felt like every day I was treading water as hard as I could, screaming for help. There was always something else that would just push me back under." Over time, Haley's experience with a highly combative female senior pastor left her "running ragged." She initially thought that she "got out just before the point of burnout. But in retrospect, I was past that point."

Feeling Decimated (physical)

The category of *feeling decimated (physical)* overlapped considerably with the previous category of *soul being chipped away (psychological),* as physical and psychological abuse were extremely intertwined within the women's experiences. The following social processes were present in increasing levels of intensity, beginning with *others needing to possess or control my body,* followed by more severe experiences of *no longer functioning,* and *just one death threat.* Similar to the social dynamics in earlier categories, the women negotiated both internalized messages and prior social conditioning as well as external messages and explicit expectations within their ministry contexts.

Others Needing to Possess or Control my Body

Throughout the interviews, the women described others wanting to control or possess their bodies, with varying levels of scrutiny ranging from over-interested to inappropriately fixated. Each of the women faced extensive commentary on a variety of aspects of their body, including their hair, clothing, shoes, earrings, makeup, and tone of their voice. The women experienced this constant feedback through varying levels of criticism, judgement, and voyeurism. The desire to possess or control the women's bodies was further magnified by others' comments and behaviors surrounding pregnancy and reproduction.

Certain parishioners showed a disturbing fastidiousness, bordering on obsession, regarding the women's bodily presentation, which was later reinforced in the social process of *gendered infantilizing*. Marta described this dynamic, noting:

> I definitely had people doing inappropriate things, touching me inappropriately. I will not say sexually at all, but in terms of touching my hair, or "let me fix your shirt" or "let me. . ." whatever it was. It was kind of like I was the grandkid. I was the kid who mommy or daddy could help touch and fix up. It bothered me, but I also sort of knew that I was not alone in that, in terms of the experience as a young clergy woman. It just kind of grated on me. I had one woman who decided that my hair was not right on Sunday mornings and always put her hands in my hair, and I had to tell her a number of times, "This is not appropriate." I finally grabbed her wrist one day when she was reaching up. And she got so mad at me. She literally did not talk to me for the rest of my time there. And I thought, you know what, this is your problem, not mine.

Miranda received a variety of comments on her style of dress. From older men, it was often sexualized with one male colleague asking, "Hey, I love the boots today, would you tell my wife where you're going shopping?" Older women would criticize her use of high heel shoes noting, "You need to be up there and people shouldn't be distracted by you. They need to come to God." Conversely, her choice of shoes while leading worship services was often celebrated by younger women, one of whom said, "I love coming forward for Communion because I want to look at your shoes." Miranda felt that her clothing choices were never meant to be offensive or to draw attention, but were a form of creative expression and spirituality. She saw her aesthetic choices as a "way into the spirit so others can see that God is more than just these rules or this black-and-white kind of vision of God." Similarly, Elsa saw that her clothing choices were seen as "permission-giving and liberating" for some and "scary and threatening" for others:

> In the winter I would wear tights, which I love to get because I wear a simple black dress every day. I'd get sort of fun patterns for my tights. And there was a man who would say "Oh, I love seeing what tights you're wearing." And it was like, I think you mean that well, but it doesn't come out well. Even my theology was liberating. And my presence was permission-giving and liberating for others and that is scary and threatening for many.

In terms of pregnancy, there was intense discussion directed at clergy women who were pregnant, nursing, trying to conceive, or not wanting to have children, which felt extremely intrusive for those who experienced it. Sandra and Marta, both of whom were married and in their early forties while in ministry, received ongoing pressure from church members to get pregnant, despite each woman expressing not wanting to have children. After being told by a female church member "If you're going to get pregnant, you're going to have to go fast," Marta responded, "Yeah, okay, thanks for telling me how my body works. I'm keenly aware of that." Sandra shared that church members "pretty obviously expected me to single handedly or 'single wombedly' populate their Sunday school. They didn't know that we weren't planning to have children and they were upset, noting 'but you promised that you would.'"

Melanie described inappropriate comments about her reproductive life as a reflection of a larger desire among some to have "possession over a clergy woman's body," which she found deeply distressing:

> I had church members who would tell me on a regular basis, "I just think that your son needs a little brother or sister." I finally got to the point where I was like, "Well, we're trying, but it's not working. Do you want to know what's going on?" And they got more information than they wanted because somehow my ability to reproduce was part of their narrative of what should

94

be happening in the church. It's not even just the role of being a mother and a pastor, but there's some sense in which church people feel some sort of possession over a clergy woman's body that I swear they don't over a clergy man.

No Longer Functioning

Each of the women described the compounded effects of emotional and physical depletion, which ultimately lead to their decisions to leave toxic ministry contexts. Psychological abuse would manifest itself in concrete physical symptoms and illness just as questions of physical safety would cause feelings of intense anxiety and emotional stress, particularly if not adequately acknowledged by the surrounding church leadership. Several women noted the ways in which the psychological abuse they experienced manifested physically to the point that they could no longer function. More severe examples are included in the later category of *life was threatened,* in which the drastic physical impact of emotional stress and psychological abuse became the deciding factor in decisions to leave.

Kay described "feeling decimated" yet unable to take medical leave because of the church's financial situation and lack of support from the denomination:

After my second year it was just going downhill really, really fast. After feeling terrible all day, I had to go to the hospital immediately after an evening meeting, which turned out to be a pulmonary embolus. I was in the hospital for the next week, and the treasurer came in and, looking back, I recognize this as such an abuse move. She had just raised her voice at me in a meeting in front of witnesses at the church and then came into the hospital the next week with a gift and note saying, "We hope you feel better." I felt like I couldn't ask for medical leave, just by the tone of voice of the denominational representative, and I ended up having a family member drive me to the church because I was just so unwell. I would preach sitting down, go home and sleep for like four hours. I was just decimated.

Vivienne described similar "physical unravelings" that alerted her to the extreme nature of what she was expected to endure. The physical effects heightened after a particularly difficult conflict with the senior pastor who, along with the church board, had refused to pay the taxes on the pastor's housing, which was part of her employment contract:

I remember the physical unraveling starting with migraines. But then I got huge sores around my eyes, and I don't even know what it was. It was some form of dermatitis that my doctor could never explain. It just erupted on my face. It was both itchy and painful. I would wake up and my eyes would be completely swollen shot. And it would just be day to day, and really painful, all from stress.

My sleep patterns were so disturbed, completely rocked. I ended up getting into long distance running, even though I was so dead tired. At least to have that rhythmic breathing, it would help reset my brain and just to be doing physical activity was good.

I was a nervous wreck to the point where I would just jump out of my skin when people would look in my office door. And it just was fatiguing to the point where my body was really unhappy. I was not functioning well.

Just One Death Threat

Just as Marta's experience of psychological abuse encapsulated the earlier category of *chipping away my soul,* Sarah's experience, noted below, is a powerful reflection of the social process of *just one death threat.* At first, Sarah's experience seemed like a possible outlier due to the highly specific and traumatic nature of two distinct death threats that she endured. However, in holding her experience up to the other interviews, it was clear that several elements were reflective of larger themes that carried across several other women's experiences.

Sarah described a male congregant, Erik, who had been previously convicted of financial fraud and was actively abusing his wife, specifically trying to push her toward suicide. Sarah provided pastoral care to his wife while she was being hospitalized in an ICU following an attempted suicide, after which Erik began stalking Sarah and pressuring the denomination for her removal. Sarah shared that eventually:

> He was picked up by the police and he was wearing a disguise. He had a backpack full of ammunition, multiple weapons, and a map of my house and my office at church. He was planning to kill me and his ex-wife. I remember the sheriff calling me when Erik had been picked up. I didn't know I had been stalked. I didn't know there was a hit list and I was on it. The authorities knew, but I didn't. As things unfolded, it was really scary.

I paused the interview for a few moments as Sarah was visibly distraught. It had been several years since the incident but the trauma of the experience was clearly still felt, even after significant therapy and her own work as a trauma-informed spiritual director.

After Erik was arrested and made bail, Sarah entered an extremely frightening period, which included court appearances, safeguarding the church, her home, and her physical body. She described what it felt like to provide leadership for a fearful congregation while at the same time being the primary target:

> On Sunday mornings I would come to church, wait in the parking lot, make sure my police escort was there, who would come in with me and then wait until I left again, just so I could literally function. I have no idea how I functioned during that time. I really had this attitude of—I'm not gonna let him chase me away from ministry. And I just kept showing up to church,

just kept doing my job, you know. I didn't really realize I had a choice but to keep leading.

Sarah felt strongly that she needed to continue serving in her role as pastor in order to prove her competence as a woman clergy and leader. She stayed several years after the initial death threat, but after she found a hole drilled in the gas tank of her car, she felt, "I can work through one death threat. Two is my limit." She described her physical and mental state following the second death threat:

> I had a month medical leave, during which I was throwing up every day. I lost about 25 pounds, because I just couldn't do it. I mean I was literally in post-traumatic stress. It wasn't just the car. I think all the stuff from before that I had just repressed and gotten through just exploded and I couldn't do it anymore. By this point I'm starting to think that I can't go back to my church. I was so angry, so hurt, but at the same time didn't want to quit. I heard a lot of "maybe you aren't cut out for this" kind of talk but I had never heard of any of colleagues going through anything remotely like what I went through.
>
> I came back to work and still felt really sick and traumatized and a colleague said, "You're just letting your anxiety get to you." And I literally resigned right there. I was like, I'm done, I can't. I felt so gaslit by the place I'd served well for so long, as if it was my fault I was "anxious," aka a severe case of PTSD. I probably should have left the first time around, but I didn't feel I was done doing ministry there. I felt I can work through one death threat. Two is my limit.

Sarah's experience reflected key themes that emerged in other clergy interviews including 1) others denying or not taking seriously a pastor's suffering; 2) clergy women feeling the need to endure suffering in order to prove their leadership competency; and 3) internalized messages and understandings of one's calling to serve at all costs, thereby minimizing feelings of intense stress and abuse. The overriding of chronic physical and psychological abuse reflects the concept of "sacrificial embrace" (Greene & Robbins, 2015), discussed earlier in Chapter 2, in which some of the women interpreted extreme conditions as inherent to the work of ministry and something they were willing to accept based on their overall sense of purpose and calling. However, over time, the women questioned their own acceptance of such abuse and mistreatment, as they identified more clearly what they could and could not tolerate.

Naming the Abuse and Trauma

The words "abuse" and "trauma" were regularly used within the interviews; however, this language was often not accessible to the women while in their ministry settings. For some of the women, naming the abuse and trauma emerged as part of their decisions to leave, while others did not use this language until undergoing professional therapy as part of their healing and recovery beyond active ministry. The key social processes included in this category are *mirroring domestic abuse, love bombing and narcissistic abuse,* and *spiritual abuse.*

Mirroring Domestic Abuse

Several women noted previous exposure to the dynamics of domestic abuse and intimate partner violence, either through work experience, educational background, or first-hand experience within abusive marriages or relationships. Allegra made a direct connection between her experiences in ministry and domestic abuse noting:

I've done some work around domestic violence because that was part of the issue in my marriage. Sometimes I felt like you're just supposed to take it. You're the woman and you're supposed to take this and we should not question it. That's the part I think that hurts the most. Sometimes I just laugh, just a release of how crazy it is that I took it for so long.

Melanie described seeing a counselor two different times due to a previous intimate relationship that was emotionally abusive. Through her work in therapy, she was able to identify that "this man had pushed some boundaries that I just had never firmly set in my life, so I knew that I had important work to do in that area." This awareness ultimately helped Melanie identify co-dependent patterns within her ministry setting that she was no longer willing to tolerate. Sandra's background in psychology and previous work at a domestic abuse response center alerted her to the abusive dynamics between herself and the congregation. She was aware of how "different types of abuse can exist in the world and how they are perpetrated. There are both physical and emotional ways that you can manipulate and control someone."

Love Bombing and Narcissistic Abuse

Just as knowledge of and direct experience with domestic abuse alerted some of the women to similar dynamics within their ministry settings, Hope's divorce from what she described as a controlling and manipulative man alerted her to the specific manipulative behaviors of church-based narcissistic abuse. Hope specifically pointed out the phenomenon of "love bombing," a type of emotional abuse where someone uses grand gestures and ingratiating communication in order to manipulate and control another person (Strutzenberg et al., 2017):

I don't think I ever really appreciated how the systems of patriarchy worked within the church. I mean, you know it's there, but until you get exposed to it and experience it firsthand and have to deal with it—it's very disorienting. From the standpoint of you always feel like church should be a safe space. It should be a place to go for healing. And it was very much that for me, for a long time. And then it became the thing that was doing harm to me. That part was hard to wrap my head around because it felt almost like when you fall in love with a narcissist and they love bomb you and then the switch flips.

When asked to describe the experience of "love bombing," Hope offered the following:

> When you go to seminary and first go into ministry, you get told so often how this is a calling, this is your vocation, and they're so excited that you're here and they're so excited that you're gonna be such a great pastor. You get kind of lulled into this sense that you're valued. You're valued up until you challenge. And the minute you start to challenge anything or you start to say, "Hey, this isn't okay," then it's like I said, that switch just flips. And then you're the problem. And you know, well, if you talk about this, we can't place you in another call.

Allegra also observed a similar shift when "stepping out of line," but more so from the vantage point of a parent-child relationship:

> Initially it feels really warm and fuzzy. Because you're like, oh look, they just love me so much. And it feeds your ego, like I'm so cool and I'm just so special, because they're telling me how special I am. But as you're going along, you're like, no, they're infantilizing me and I'm a child to them. I'm not an adult and I'm not their pastor. I am the representation of their own children for them in their mind. And if I step out of line, then that's when there are going to be problems. Whatever that line is for them. And so that feels awful because there's a lack of respect, and also not being seen as an equal or even as a leadership presence because you're seen as just a child.

Spiritual Abuse

In addition to domestic abuse and narcissistic abuse, several of the women described an overarching spiritual abuse. Sandra described overlapping layers of abuse that she experienced as a clergy woman, which she placed under the larger umbrella of spiritual abuse:

My experience in ministry had the same hallmarks of isolation and gaslighting, discrediting, and scapegoating, all of the hallmarks of every other type of abuse. It's just that this one was couched in theological language. It just seems to me like emotional abuse that happens in the church almost inherently becomes spiritual abuse. If somebody is physically abused in the church that is also spiritual abuse because a trusted leader has taken advantage of somebody in a place where they were supposed to feel the presence of God, and instead they feel the presence of an abuser. And violence is done to them instead of spiritual growth. I would just say any type of abuse that happens in a church or a faith community setting, ends up being spiritual abuse as well as whatever other type it might be.

LaVerne described spiritual abuse as taking advantage of one's passion to serve. She shared a devastating example of a young male colleague who she felt was "being pimped for his passion," and placed in a very precarious and underpaid call setting that left him unable to physically care for himself:

It's literally disgusting that the church even years after I've left is in the same space. That it drains you. It can kill you. It doesn't care that you're dead. It wasn't something you can make a living with, and needing to take on other jobs. It took a lot of your time. It took a lot of your money. It took a lot of your energy. And he never came to terms with that. His health started to deteriorate. . . and they found them dead, just laid out on the ground. And he was probably in his early forties. They pimped him for his passion. Legit took advantage of it.

Jenny initially felt hesitant to use the word "abuse" but ultimately felt that the church institution "empowers abuse":

I don't think that these people are bad people, and I think that's the hard thing. I think that the institution of the church, the way that it's structured and the theology that has been passed down in recent decades, empowers abuse. It makes it so that's the only way that people know how to interact with their pastor is in abusive ways. And then it's sanctioned by the church. No institution is stellar at this. But I feel like if you go into the secular world, there are definitions for abuse. There is a sense for what appropriate language is, and appropriate behavior. But I don't feel like that exists at all in the church.

I feel guilty using the word "abuse" and at the same time I know that that's what I've experienced. I felt like all I could do was continually offer myself as a lamb for slaughter because I couldn't get away from them. I had to keep standing up there making myself a target every Sunday morning. I felt theologically abused the way I was emotionally, psychologically, and verbally abused by people. And I just wrote it off, just took it. I was taking up my cross. I feel coming out of the church, I'm finding myself in a way that I had completely lost. I can see how I was treated terribly for a long time.

Shadow Side of Servant-Leadership

The overarching categories of *experiencing feminized servanthood as dehumanizing* and *experiencing feminized servanthood as abusive* reveal the highly gendered nature of service-oriented leadership and expose the often hidden and harmful elements of models of "servant-leadership" (Greenleaf, 2002). Initially presented in leadership scholarship as a social good that promotes moral integrity, self-reflective humility, and care for the needs of others both within and beyond organizational structures, servant-leadership has the capacity to reorient hierarchical institutions of power toward more human-centered approaches to leadership (Greenleaf, 2002). However, as evidenced in this study, such understandings of servant-leadership are oversimplified and idealized in ways that fail to address imbedded gender narratives of power and servitude, and societal expectations of the self-sacrificial woman.

Eicher-Catt (2005) exposed the gendered nature of servant-leadership, revealing that the juxtaposition of the terms "servant" and "leader" lead to a "mythical theology of leadership for organizational life that upholds androcentric patriarchal norms" (p. 17). Feminist scholars continue to critique the inherent gender bias within models of servant-leadership arguing that the relational focus on downplaying self-promotion and prioritizing forgiveness and "interpersonal acceptance," accentuate gender bias in ways that lead to damaging levels of altruism and selflessness (Reynolds, 2014, p. 42). Promoting narratives of self-denial are particularly harmful for women leaders, especially within social contexts where women have historically been invisibilized within caregiving and sacrificial roles.

As illustrated by the clergy women's experiences, the shadow side of servant-leadership emerges through the interplay of three concrete factors: 1) unsustainable expectations of pastoral job performance particularly with regard to physical and emotional availability; 2) gendered expectations of the self-sacrificial woman, which involved both internalized messages and social conditioning experienced by the clergy woman as well surrounding gender narratives of feminized servanthood; and 3) "sacrificial embrace" (Greene & Robbins, 2015), in which a clergy woman's own understanding of purpose and calling as a pastor caused her to endure, override, or minimize acute and prolonged exposure to psychological abuse. These three areas are illustrated in Figure 4.3, which highlights how these elements mutually informed each other, ultimately producing the damaging social dynamics of *feminized servanthood as dehumanizing and abusive.*

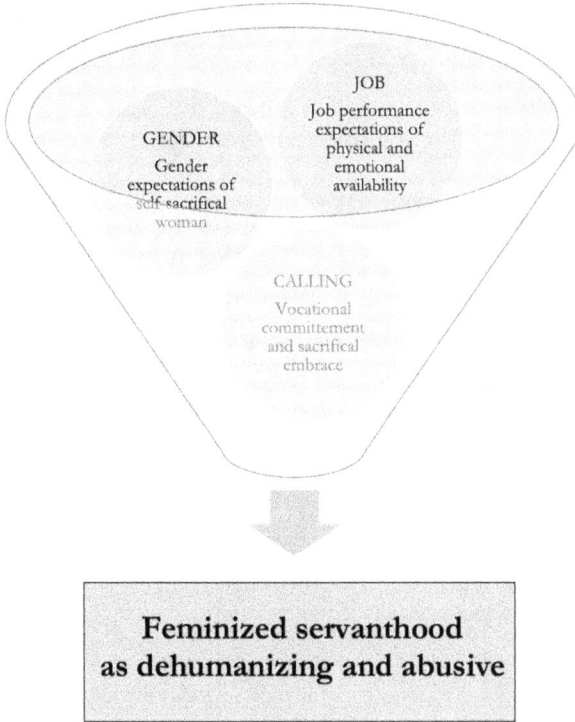

GENDER

Gender
expectations of
self-sacrifical
woman

JOB

Job performance
expectations of
physical and
emotional
availability

CALLING

Vocational
committement
and sacrifical
embrace

**Feminized servanthood
as dehumanizing and abusive**

Copyright 2024 by Lynn M. Horan

*Figure 4.3: The Shadow Side of Servant-Leadership for Protestant
Clergy Women*

The interrelated dynamics of job expectations, gender expectations, and calling or "sacrificial embrace" (Greene & Robbins, 2015) were shared throughout the women's experiences. Cindy described the intense job expectations of emotional availability, noting:

As pastors, we were taught to be the non-anxious presence and then do our processing apart from that moment and accept that things would happen within us and that was something to be processed on our own. No one else was going to ever alter their behavior. It was always on me, to be the person changing my behavior or at least sort of protecting my own psychological safety.

Deborah described the unsustainability of addressing conflicting congregational needs as a never-ending game of "blind whack-a-mole." In many ways, this image foreshadows the reversed dynamic, in which the clergy women themselves became the targeted "mole" or contagion to remove.

> The people there had such different expectations of me and I was sort of playing blind whack-a-mole trying to figure out what people were expecting, what people were saying, never knowing quite what people needed or just knowing that the needs were different. We had people who expected a community organizer and visionary leader who was always out in the community. But that really rubbed against other people's expectations that I would always be visiting them personally in their home and talking to them on a daily basis and attending to their very constant needs.

As one moves through the pressurized system of feminized servanthood illustrated above, the second component addresses gendered expectations of the self-sacrificial woman. This element of feminized servanthood ranged from people-pleasing and over-functioning to feelings of invisibility as the ultimate expression of the self-sacrificial woman. Deborah addressed this compounded dynamic and damaging dual expectations of being a service-oriented pastor and self-sacrificial woman, noting:

> There's this assumption that if you're in leadership in the denomination and especially if you're a woman, you suck it up and take the insult and the stress. And it's your job as a leader to be the one who absorbs it. But it lands more heavily on the women in the system than it does on the men. There's an assumption that the pastor has to suck it up in all these instances of boundary crossing. And as a woman, we're not allowed to say "this is enough."

The combination of service-oriented pastoral leadership and gendered expectations of the self-sacrificial woman was further complicated by the third feature of "sacrificial embrace" (Greene & Robbins, 2015), in which one overrides or normalizes instances of acute and/or chronic psychological abuse due to a strong sense of vocational calling. Sarah described the gendered aspects of sacrificial embrace in the midst of not one but two death threats, in which she felt she had to prove her leadership by staying at the church for several more years amid debilitating fear and anxiety:

This was not minor harassment or somebody not liking my sermon. This was so much bigger and literally life-threatening, but I think, how old was I? I was in my thirties. I thought, no, I'm a powerful young woman, you know? We almost have to be, we have to be invincible to prove our leadership, our worth as a public leader. I look back now and think that's ridiculous but I was still new enough that I didn't want people to think I couldn't hack it. But this was not the situation of "not hacking it," it was an attempt on my life.

Cindy reflected similar elements of vocational calling that were reinforced in an unhealthy way theologically:

I didn't grow up particularly religious, so I definitely didn't grow up with that expectation. But in college I had my sort of becoming a Christian moment and I do think some of the attitudes deeply affected me, like being extreme and grandiose and the idea that you should be willing to do anything for the sake of the call. And I really bought into that kind of need to be willing to give up anything. To follow what God wants for me. And even when my theology shifted away from evangelicalism, I think the denial of self had really taken hold of me.

As the women negotiated the three-pronged dynamic of feminized servanthood (unsustainable job expectations, harmful gender narratives, and strong vocational calling), there was an increased feeling that the physical and psychological impact was not only dehumanizing but abusive in ways the clergy women could no longer tolerate. The women's experiences revealed how gendered expectations of servant-leadership harm women leaders in concrete and damaging ways (see Figure 4.4). This shadow side of servant-leadership is evident not only in religious contexts with theologically embedded narratives of self-sacrifice but also non-religious caregiving sectors such as healthcare and education, as well as corporate sectors with highly gendered roles and expectations.

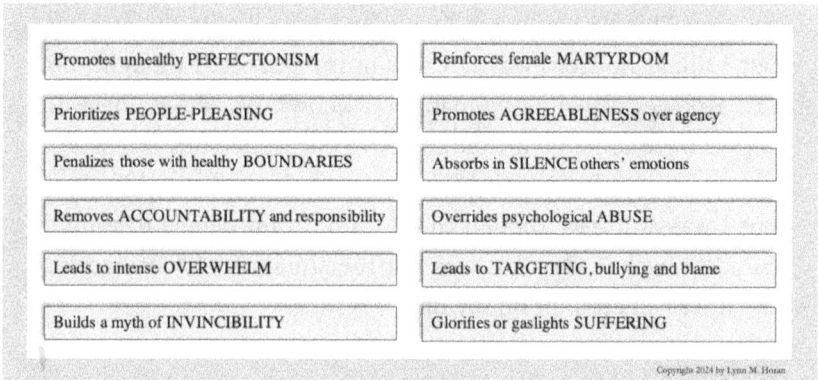

Promotes unhealthy PERFECTIONISM	Reinforces female MARTYRDOM
Prioritizes PEOPLE-PLEASING	Promotes AGREEABLENESS over agency
Penalizes those with healthy BOUNDARIES	Absorbs in SILENCE others' emotions
Removes ACCOUNTABILITY and responsibility	Overrides psychological ABUSE
Leads to intense OVERWHELM	Leads to TARGETING, bullying and blame
Builds a myth of INVINCIBILITY	Glorifies or gaslights SUFFERING

Copyright 2024 by Lynn M. Horan

Figure 4.4: Consequences of Feminized Servanthood and the Shadow Side of Servant-Leadership

Having presented the overarching dimensions of *feminized servanthood as dehumanizing* and *feminized servanthood as abusive,* the remainder of this chapter and the following two chapters will outline four additional primary dimensions evident in the research findings (see Table 4.1 above). These areas include 1) *differentiating self from system;* 2) *exposing vs. protecting toxic leaders and harmful systems;* 3) *nail in the coffin;* and 4) *reconstituting self.*

DIFFERENTIATING SELF FROM SYSTEM

Amid the highly gendered expectations and psychological abuse within the clergy women's ministry contexts, there were important opportunities where each clergy woman was able to enact agency and self-actualization based on her own understanding of pastoral leadership. These areas of agency were reflected in the primary dimension of *differentiating self from system*, in which the women actively negotiated and responded to the surrounding culture of feminized servanthood. Amid this back-and-forth interplay, conflicting gender narratives converged and sometimes collided with the participants' various expressions of self-differentiation. Table 4.4 illustrates the primary dimension of *differentiating self from system*, which includes the categories of *negotiating expectations and boundaries, decentralizing leadership,* and *conflicting gender narratives*.

Primary Dimension	Conceptual Categories and Corresponding Social Processes		
Differentiating Self from System	**Negotiating Expectations and Boundaries** • Porous boundaries • Buffering bullshit • Unspoken and double-bind expectations	**Decentralizing Leadership** • Equipping others and sharing power • Meeting people where they are • Bringing people to the table	**Conflicting Gender Narratives** • Gendered infantilizing • Mother-daughter wound • Disrupting masculinity

Table 4.4: Primary Dimension: Differentiating Self from System

Negotiating Expectations and Boundaries

As noted earlier, self-differentiation is a relational practice in which one is able to identify with another person's emotional state, yet at the same time maintain an awareness that "the source of the affect is in the other" (Jordan, 1991, p. 69). This practice is essential in pastoral leadership as one balances empathy with appropriate boundaries. The women described self-differentiation in various ways, including Marta and Cindy determining whether something or someone was "not my circus," and choosing to disengage. Sarah described self-differentiation as "being able to leave the room and I am still intact":

Early in ministry I felt like a waitress saying, "Tell me every-thing that you want and I will fill your order." And now I just think not everybody is going to be happy and that's okay. My approach to leadership now is very much grounded in being whole, of being able to come in and minister to somebody but not take on their stuff. It's being able to leave the room and I am still intact. I haven't given away pieces of myself. It takes a lot of self-awareness of what am I bringing in that's my stuff and owning that.

Intentionally differentiating oneself from the surrounding social system, enabled the women to employ strong relational skills when engaging with others. However, as the women applied various strate-gies for maintaining and protecting their interpersonal boundaries, they also faced significant resistance and push-back from those who were more enmeshed within toxic church systems.

Porous Boundaries

Each of the women described the overall conditions of their ministry contexts as having extremely blurred boundaries, both between staff members and clergy as well as between clergy and parishioners. Deborah, who went from a large multi-staff church to a smaller congregation, described the familial nature of porous boundaries:

I moved to a much smaller congregation in a neighboring state, which had a totally different dynamic. They had had a female pastor before. It's a much more progressive area and the dynamic of a small congregation meant that there were more porous boundaries between me as the pastor and them as congregants. So, a lot of boundary crossing happened I think because they saw me as their daughter or granddaughter or friend, instead of professional whom they pay to do a certain job.

Sandra described porous boundaries within her ministry context, in which the congregation enabled the senior pastor's well-known misconduct, with complicit church board members being protected by the larger congregation. Within this context of loyalty and dysfunction, Sandra felt that:

Accountability was never an option because the senior pastor was so charismatic and so many people liked him and just for that reason they didn't care if he did anything, they just wanted his personality. Holding him accountable was never an option because the church board members were his friends and didn't want to be his supervisors. Even though they actually were his supervisors, they weren't willing to be.

Buffering Bullshit

There was an ongoing feedback loop in which the women would experience boundary violations causing the woman to need to protect or maintain their boundaries, followed by parishioners' emotional projection and reactivity to those established boundaries. It was often described by the women as an extremely messy process of negotiation, with both internal questioning over what battles one should or could fight, and external negotiation with those who exhibited antagonizing behaviors. Cindy described her role in this dynamic as "buffering bullshit," while Melanie described boundary-setting as:

Being able to recognize that I have limitations and needs. That I don't need to bleed into what everyone else or who everyone else is, and what everyone else needs. And kind of vice versa. I am a person who has my own life and needs my own space.

Jenny often felt the need to coach parishioners on the concept of emotional projection, particularly in their treatment of other church members. Unfortunately, these efforts at conflict-resolution were often not well-received:

If someone got mad there was always something else under the surface but the person couldn't talk about it in a way that was decipherable. One of the board members got mad because the organist's husband died and she heard about it in the grocery store. I said, "You can't get mad at the organist for not telling you first. She's grieving and this isn't about you." Three days later this person just rage quit the church board.

Unspoken and Double-Bind Expectations

There were multiple layers of spoken and unspoken expectations that the women experienced, which related to both job performance and pastoral responsibilities as well as the perpetuation of specific gender roles and behaviors. The women struggled to navigate this system of overt and implicit social rules, overlapping and often contradictory messages, and rigid ways of being that were not reflective of their self-understanding and approach to leadership. Hope described the inability to navigate this constant tension noting:

In my case, it was a bunch of double bind expectations and things that started off as, "Why are you out in the community? You should be in the office more. Oh, you're in the office. Why aren't you out there more?" It was all those double-bind expectations where you can never win.

Cindy described the constant need to "nimbly shift between roles" and the impossibility of satisfying everyone's unspoken needs:

There were often really high expectations of this kind of multi-level relationship with the pastor, which wasn't unique to me. As I talked to people, what they wanted from all of their pastors was for them to be constantly able to shift between being their best friend, not just a friend, but like their best, their closest friend, and their therapist and a spiritual leader. And being able to nimbly shift between all of those roles all the time, but to be the idealized spiritual leader who was never going to tell them that they could be better. So, I experienced a lot of that and it was kind of at the crux of when I was getting to the worst part of my time there.

The women also consistently shared the unspoken expectation of needing to be a mind-reader, particularly around health needs and hospitalizations of older congregants. Melanie described a woman who was extremely angry that she didn't visit her husband in the hospital after surgery:

> But she hadn't told anybody until after the surgery had even happened. I can't read minds but it was definitely like "Melanie is not taking care of the old sick people enough and that's all we want her to do."

This demand for constant availability was also extended to Sandra, who described the "expectation that I work more hours than I was working. It didn't matter how many hours I was working, but there was always the expectation that I wasn't working enough." These experiences of boundary negotiation called upon the clergy women to exercise highly evolved leadership skills and emotional intelligence, which reflected the women's own self-differentiation from the surrounding system.

Decentralizing Leadership

The category of *decentralizing leadership* was a particularly strong area of discernment, decision-making, and agency as the women collaborated with other clergy, church leaders, and parishioners as well as the surrounding community outside of the church walls. While there was significant support for this form of bridge-building leadership, the women also faced ongoing pushback as their collaborative leadership approaches were seen by some as a threat to dominant narratives of authority and power-over models. The specific pathways of agency and intentional leadership practices are illustrated by the social processes of *equipping others and sharing power, bringing people to the table* and *meeting people where they are.*

Equipping Others and Sharing Power

The women noted several ways in which they would equip others and share power within their ministry contexts, using such language as "inclusivity," "collaboration," "shared vision," and "power with." Several women noted that their collaborative approaches with other clergy, staff, and church members, were often received with question, uncertainty, or rejection among those who promoted more unilateral or top-down approaches of leadership and authority.

Hope, an associate pastor, noted the congregation's discussion as to whether she wanted to apply for the senior pastor's position after his retirement. Having no interest in the position, Hope noted:

"If it's a pastor that I can work with and we have a shared vision," I said, "I'm all for it." Which apparently was completely bizarre to them. They were like, oh, having a senior and associate that would share a vision of what should happen at the church? Huh. And I was like, "Yeah, how else does it work?"

Melanie described a similar desire to work collaboratively and took great care to work with the church board to clarify job descriptions, noting, "From the get go, I said you cannot give someone a terrible evaluation and try to get them to quit just because you don't like one thing about them." Haley described her collaborative style as "prioritizing different things" than the older White male leadership of the congregation who she felt "talked down to her":

I work a little differently than they expected their pastor to work. I prioritize different things. I prioritize children. I don't prioritize my own ego in an unhealthy way. And my tendency to ask questions before making assertions. My tendency to not present things as if I have the answer. My collaborative style was, I think, always perceived as weakness or insecurity or timidity.

Deborah described her collaborative approach to leadership as "a lot of conversation and assuming wisdom is in the gathered body. I'm not the expert in the room." This was in contrast to the male senior pastor who she felt had been "formed to be the leader, the one in charge who made all the decisions, and that was not how the system worked in the congregation." Similarly, Allegra described her leadership approach of equipping others as "empowering communal voice," a practice that she deeply valued but also enacted out of necessity due to others' inability to hear and respect her:

Some folks were hard, so how I would work with that is I would use the communal group to speak for something instead of using my own voice. I would check in with the conversation and then I would try to guide the conversation a little bit. But when that person would just be that person, what I found in those situations is that when it came from their peers it was a lot harder for them to argue against it. But if it came from me and my voice, it was so easy for them to tear it down.

Other participants noted such approaches as "complementing others' visions," not wanting to be a "woman alone on an island," "showing a united front," "thinking of possibilities not just problems," "trying hard not to be a rigid person," and "visioning as seeing the big picture and the little details in order to move forward."

Bringing People to the Table

The women expressed various ways of building relationships and partnering with others, both within their respective congregations as well as in the surrounding community. Christy described her inclusive leadership style as "bringing people to the table," particularly with regard to affirming the LGBTQ+ community:

> I think that who I am as a leader is someone who wants more people at the table. I think because of that I had a really large spectrum of people I was a pastor to, because that's my job. There's a lot of really conservative culty churches in this area and that was another reason why I wanted to go there because it's such a witness to be the progressive church in kind of a desert land. I actually want to sit down at the table with people and talk to them. To be in relationship with others so much so that we might change our minds too.

Other women shared examples of building relationships and partnering with others beyond their immediate congregations. Miranda described the process of being a "catalyst for connection," particularly with other regional churches and clergy. Having felt that nobody was reaching out to her, it was important for Miranda's own psychological well-being to ask others "'How are you doing? What's going on in your church? What do you do? How can we pray for each other?' But people just get really busy and they get in their silos." Jenny was also very committed to building relationships with the larger community, but faced resistance within her congregation in the form of "passive engagement":

> I wanted to offer activities that would fill needs in the community and connect them to the church and to really think outside the box about what church looks like. But the church was just really passively engaged. So that the whole thing had to be conceived of and implemented by me. It was just exhausting.

An important part of bringing people to the table and partnering with others also extended to creative ways of using the church building, which was often received with caution, suspicion, and/or rejection from within the congregation. Kay, a solo pastor, worked with the church board to open the doors of the church for the community to use during a significant flood, which led to conflict with the church's facility manager. Christy explored offering building space for a local AA group and opening the church's playground to the larger community, noting "What does our table look like? Is our table letting our building be used? I think it should be."

Meeting People Where They Are

The women noted having perceptive forms of communication, in which they utilized highly nuanced aspects of emotional intelligence in order to assess where people were within a particular conversation or conflict. Haley described how she applied this intentional approach to conflict resolution:

I built it over time. I had a challenging family life growing up. I had an older brother who had anger management issues. And I was the peacemaker. So that was part of it, I think. I also worked with developmentally disabled adults in my early career before ministry. And then also worked with children and not to equate the two, not to infantilize people with disabilities, but having to meet someone where they are and figure out what's going on with them and how to find some common understanding and get everybody's needs met. I've built that skill set over time and have also taken workshops on mediation and nonviolent communication.

Deborah, an associate pastor, noted:

I think one my skills is attentiveness to the emotional sense in a room. Understanding what's happening in the collective emotion. Being able to tell that the vibe is changing. Like, we should pause and pay attention to what is happening. Something's going on, somebody over there in the corner is upset.

Marta described the process of meeting people where they are as offering "teaching moments that also show empathy":

> I think sometimes being a woman gives you a greater sense of empathy, not always. The parish associate that I love dearly is a man and has one of the greatest senses of empathy. Empathy has carried me forward and it helps me, particularly in teaching and training deacons [who do pastoral care visits]. I love finding teaching moments that also show empathy, and those end up combining in terms of strengths.

Allegra found that an important part of her leadership was understanding family system dynamics, which for some of the clergy women was part of their seminary training and/or denominational training around interpersonal boundaries:

> My training in family systems became a strength for me because I was able to look at what was happening in different churches and different systems and say, okay, who is the identified patient here? Who are they willing to listen to? What is the history behind this? Has this conversation happened before? Who are they identifying me as?

While working with a highly combative and reactive older female senior pastor, Haley described her intentional approach to conflict resolution. This description relates strongly to the earlier category of *absorbing others' emotions,* however, Haley felt that taking on the "emotional labor" within a relational dynamic served as both a leadership strength and at times a method of survival:

> My thought process was always like, this person is really activated and is saying things that are extremely reactive. Engaging with them as they are is not going to lead to a resolution that is satisfactory for either of us. And I need to defuse this and then sort of shepherd us along. Do the emotional labor of processing

this interaction that we've had, this conflict, what's at stake for each of us, what kind of outcome would be agreeable so that we can preserve this working relationship. And she just was not willing to do that. I explained this to the denominational leadership at one point noting that I have really good conflict skills and she was just not having any of it and was just actively antagonizing me. I wasn't taking the bait and that made her even more mad.

Melanie offered an additional nuance, noting that her approach to intentional communication and conflict resolution was not about making everyone happy:

I had a male church member who was very caring and supportive of me who said, "I just want to help you make everyone happy so you can stay here as long as possible." And I started pretty early saying to him, "That's not why I'm here. I'm not here to make everyone happy."

Marta also understood the importance of self-accountability, which she did not experience from other leaders in her ministry context. She felt it was important to "apologize for my role in something because to me that's what you do. That's the mature thing to do when you've made an error, you apologize and work it out."

Conflicting Gender Narratives

An important element of differentiating oneself from the larger church system, involved conscious and deliberate agency on the part of each woman clergy as she navigated gender expectations that did not align with her own self-understanding and approaches to leadership. Each of the women experienced varying degrees of resistance to her own practices of self-differentiation, which were reflected in the social processes of *gendered infantilizing, mother-daughter wound,* and *disrupting masculinity.*

Gendered Infantilizing

The process of *gendered infantilizing* came from multiple directions, including both men and women who were congregants, senior pastors, other church staff, and denominational leaders. During the interviews, the women clergy often shared not feeling young themselves, as many entered the ministry in their mid-thirties with prior professional experience. LaVerne, a solo pastor and judicatory leader within a predominantly Black denomination, noted that a female denominational leader's decision to make her co-dean as opposed to dean was driven by both sexism and ageism:

> Because I had more education than most pastors in the denomination, she gave me the opportunity to serve in positions that some people take 20 or 30 years to get to. I use the word "co" because the politics of it was because at twenty-five, I was young. The man who was co-dean with me had no experience in pastoring. I think he just finished his seminary degree, but he was in his forties at the time. And he was a guy. I mean, that's all it boiled down to. He was a pastor, and he was a guy, but I ended up doing all the work.

Allegra's experience of being verbally attacked by an older male clergy at a denominational meeting, revealed strong elements of gendered infantilization:

> We can disagree, but you don't have to do it aggressively, like an assault. It felt like I was being "put in my place" if I'm really being honest. Like you need to be "put" somewhere, you're getting out of your place young lady. Get back in your place.

Haley noted that infantilization operated across her intersectional identities, particularly with her decision to not fully disclose her nonbinary identity as a self-protective measure within her ministry context:

Part of my not being totally out professionally is knowing that there's a great social sigma, particularly for AFAB [assigned female at birth] people who have a nonbinary identity. There's a lot of infantilization, with that. Particularly of teenage girls who are AFAB people. But I think even with just a young woman of any age, it gets infantilized. And I just did not want to give people any more reason to not take me seriously. Or any more reason to think that I'm high maintenance. it's a self-protective thing that does relate to being not taken seriously as a young woman to begin with.

Allegra described the process of "seeing through" and observing underlying social dynamics, which was initially celebrated by others as a leadership strength but later considered problematic by some due to their perception of her as a child:

I'm really good at observing people and behaviors and kind of figuring out at least a beginning of what's happening. But I want them to tell their own story. Initially people are really drawn to that in a church setting. But as it's going along they're like "Oh gosh, she's too powerful, we need to shut that down. She sees right through me and that feels uncomfortable. On the surface I wanted her to be my pastor but really she's like my kid, so I can't have her looking through me and seeing me."

Gendered infantilizing was often expressed through others' assumptions that a clergy woman "had no knowledge" or "didn't know what she was talking about." Haley remembers feeling her thoughts and ideas being discounted until someone else in the room made the same point:

There were so many meetings where I was saying something and people weren't processing it somehow and then it would be said by someone else and then it was a good idea. It made me feel insane and made me feel like it was a gaslighting experience. I later read a study of CEO boardrooms where when women talk, there's a huge percentage of the time the first thing that is said after that is some guy either restating what they just said or undermining it in some way even if they agree. And that felt so resonant.

Melanie described similar experiences of her leadership "not being taken seriously":

When I began my second appointment, an older man in the church was taking my husband and me around town introducing us to some people, including the editor of the local newspaper who said "Well, they told me she was pregnant. I didn't know she looked like she was 12 years old." And I felt the same thing within the congregation, the people who never really let me be their pastor in the first place. They may have come to church, but they didn't see me as their spiritual leader. I remember feeling, "How do I even preach to these people?" I definitely had a sense of, I'm gonna try to end well for the people who do still support me and who do still take my leadership seriously and look to me as a spiritual leader.

Undermining a clergy woman's knowledge and competence was experienced by both LaVerne and Marta who had a significant amount of education in comparison to their male colleagues, including Doctor of Ministry degrees, which is the highest level of ministry education. Marta felt being treated like a child stemmed from her intellect being "intimidating" and "threatening" to both of the senior pastors with whom she worked. Yet she distinctly felt, "I'm not going to deny that I'm smart and I'm intelligent, and my congregations have known it."

Mother-Daughter Wound

Throughout the interviews, the women shared experiences of intergenerational conflict between themselves and certain older women parishioners and clergy, typically between the ages of 60 and 75. Discussed further below, this "mother-daughter wound" relates to generational asymmetry, internalized sexism, and conflicting gender identity narratives between different generations of women (Hasseldine, 2017). Conflict was felt in a variety of different relational dyads, including the clergy women's interactions with female senior pastors and denominational leaders, staff members, particularly administrative assistants and music directors, as well as women congregants. Women who were critical of a clergy woman's leadership included both highly educated professionals who identified as politically progressive, as well as women who were more socially conservative and reflected more traditional gender roles.

Joanna, a senior pastor and head of staff, described an antagonistic relationship with an older female staff member, which Joanna attributed to elements of emotional neglect and familial conflict within the woman's childhood:

> I experienced various levels of disrespect and undermining my ministry, as well as pretty high levels of expectation, especially from one staff member. I didn't know about the concept of the "mother wound" until very recently, maybe in the last couple of years, and I'm pretty sure that's some of the dynamics there. She has sisters, her father died when she was very young. And I just suspect she spent a lot of her time pitting her sisters against each other to see who she should get on her side. If she didn't feel you were on her "team," then you were against her.

Allegra described the dynamic of the "parentified daughter" and expectations of her as a compliant helper, which caused some to strongly reject her pastoral authority:

> Every home has cultures that children have to live into, particularly daughters. I'm the oldest of three sisters, so I have always been the helper. And I've always been the peacemaker. In my own family, I functioned as a third parent in my household to

my younger siblings. So, people in the church identify that pretty quickly. They could sniff it. So, here's an oldest daughter coming in, you know, it's different than the guys, right? She can help us but she can also fit into these roles that we have in our own families and our own system.

What becomes a complication is that when I have to exert authority as a daughter, it becomes a cognitive dissonance, because children "aren't supposed to speak out against their parents." At least in some contexts, right? When I would exert authority, that's when things would get mean and nasty.

While Allegra experienced being seen as a daughter who "stepped out of line" when she exhibited agency and authority, Cindy described an older female congregant explicitly stating that she expected Cindy to be "her mother," which reveals a complicated role reversal within this dynamic:

She stormed into my office on a Sunday morning after church and screamed at me about how she expected me to be her mother and what the church expected of me was to be maternal. She was so angry at me for not fulfilling that role, for not being what she saw as motherly. Which, by the way, has never been an aspiration of mine. I am not a mother. I've never wanted to be anyone's mother, especially not my 75-year-old congregant's mother. And I did not feel like I had any particular way to respond to her and the amount of anger that she was giving me and to protect myself from that. My personal form of protection in normal life would be to tell someone that they're not allowed to speak to me that way. But as a female pastor, I had been penalized for expressing any kind of anger, which I think was really psychologically damaging in hindsight.

Miranda experienced significant animosity from an older female staff member who was frustrated because she couldn't become a priest. Miranda noted, "My existence was threatening to her and that's what I get from a lot of the older women. Either they had their own dreams that were squashed or they're just kind of old school." Allegra described similar criticism and judgement from the church's treasurer, a highly educated and self-identified feminist who would incessantly monitor her by "walking down the hall and checking in on me to make sure I was doing things properly and correctly, to make sure I was staying in line."

Conflicting gender-identity narratives between the clergy women and certain Baby Boomer women was a constant reality, particularly around childrearing and the role of children in the life of the church. The clergy women who were also mothers of young children felt distinct judgement surrounding their personal choices from older women congregants who may not have been afforded the same agency and freedom of opportunity during their personal and professional lives. Melanie, a solo pastor, felt resentment from older women in the congregation regarding her maternity leave, which has only recently become a standard policy within most mainline Protestant denominations:

> When I had my first child, I had people who were surprised that I didn't take him to church, saying, "We didn't know you were gonna hide him away." I'm like, "Well, he's a newborn baby." And then there were other women who said, "Well, I didn't get eight weeks of maternity leave when I had a child," and I'm like, "Well, sorry, but I did."

Melanie also felt a disconnect between some women congregants' over interest in her newborn child and later comments about her children's participation in worship that made her feel her children "were never really welcome at the church, like they were just a complication for me."

Joanna described a strong generational difference between the reaction of a Millennial female staff member and a retired Baby Boomer clergy woman regarding Joanna's concerns over sexual harassment from a male church member:

I ended up giving a speech in a staff meeting and said, "There's nothing to be done about this, but basically so and so is handsy so watch out," sort of like 1950's secretaries sitting around together talking. And that was where the reactions got very interesting. A woman who was a Millennial staff member said, "Why didn't you say something?" Which at that point I don't think I really solidified that it was a freeze response. I just know I didn't say anything. I also had a Baby Boomer parish associate who said, "He just touched you there? That's all?" Like, what are you worried about, that's happened a million times. And it probably did. She was one of the first women to go through seminary in the denomination. She was well into her seventies at that point and I'm sure she had a significant amount of that kind of harassment and she just didn't really understand why I had been so concerned about it.

Melanie identified two overlapping factors influencing the "push back" she received from older women including certain women needing to hold onto their authority and at the same time feeling threatened by different ways of seeing the world:

I feel like I almost always got the most push back from women, usually women in their late fifties or sixties. Some of them had a certain level of authority within the church as committee chairs or had some sort of lay leadership. And I don't know if they felt threatened by having a clergy person who was also a female or if maybe we just really disagreed on the way we saw the world.

Disrupting Masculinity

Alongside the conflicting gender narratives between different generations of women, a related social process of *disrupting masculinity* was evident among certain men who appeared to hold a particular narrative of masculinity. The clergy women sensed that the men were threatened or somehow destabilized by the various levels of agency, autonomy, and authority that the women exhibited in their pastoral roles. While the intergenerational conflict between women related specifically to the Baby Boomer generation, the men who reacted negatively to the women in this study also included those close in age to the clergy women or slightly older.

Joanna observed high-levels of anxiety among certain men within her congregation who felt that her very presence would disrupt their experience of manhood. This became evident during her final interview with elected church leaders:

> The first interview question I received was, "With the feminization of the church, do you intend to dismantle the men's group?" I had no idea what that question meant but I came to understand. When I came in as the senior pastor of that particular church, I was overseeing an all-female pastoral staff. I didn't intend to dismantle the men's group, though it was made clear that I was never welcome.

Sandra observed that the resistance to her leadership by men wasn't necessarily from older men, but from those closer to her age who seemed to feel that she threatened their masculine narrative of superiority:

> In my first two pastoral positions, I ended up working with six different older male senior pastors. The older retired ones were the most affirming and the younger ones were the most judgmental and least open, least willing to communicate, and least supportive of anything that I did.

Allegra felt resistance from the male music director who was roughly her age, as well as the older male senior pastor who dismissed her request for intervention as the head of staff:

The music director constantly felt threatened by me and would try to undermine me. He's about my age. And I remember bringing that to the head-of-staff pastor at the time who said, "Well, what do you want me to do about it?" I said, "I don't know, be his boss and say knock it off. That's what I would do." But he persisted with, "What do you want me to do about it?"

Joan, who had raised concerns about a mold infestation in the church building, described a disturbing interaction with a church board member who attempted to protect his public image as a well-known businessman by verbally attacking her:

At one of my last meetings where I came forward about what was happening and asked for help, he yelled at me. Nobody ever said to me, "We're gonna sue you." But it was that relational dynamic that caused all the anxiety for me. He had a very reactive personality. And I spent much more time trying to care for his wife and his daughter then I spent with him personally. His daughter had an eating disorder, and there was a lot happening that caused his wife to get professional help because she herself was really struggling. I think that was a threat to his public persona and so he really wanted it kept quiet.

The women navigated these social dynamics not intentionally seeking to undermine male leadership or threaten certain narratives of masculinity. Oftentimes, it was their very presence in a position of leadership that was most threatening, particularly when the clergy women promoted increased transparency, accountability, and direct communication to promote conflict resolution, as noted in the earlier conceptual category of *decentralizing leadership*. More extreme elements of toxic masculinity are described in the following chapter related to *exposing toxic leaders and harmful systems*.

"DISSIDENT DAUGHTER" AND "EMASCULATING DISRUPTOR"

As the clergy women faced ongoing resistance, it became evident that the conflict went beyond the women's specific leadership practices and reflected deep-rooted opposition to the women's presence and personhood, particularly if they exhibited self-differentiation and agency within their pastoral role. As noted above, the women described two consistent profiles of individuals who seemed most threatened, disturbed, destabilized, or otherwise uncomfortable when encountering their collaborative leadership practices and expressions of personal autonomy. These profiles included 1) certain older women with internalized sexism who perceived the clergy woman as a "dissident daughter" and 2) certain socially insecure men with rigid understandings of their own masculinity who perceived the clergy women as an "emasculating disruptor." The alliance between these specific profiles and their resulting antagonistic behavior significantly impacted the clergy women's psychological safety and was often the catalyst for the women's eventual removal or expedited resignation from their pastoral leadership positions.

The women in this study did not see themselves as being deliberately disruptive or exhibiting dissident behaviors, particularly in light of their intentionally collaborative and inclusive leadership approaches. Instead, negative perceptions of the clergy women developed when their relational and leadership approaches did not reflect others' need for female self-sacrifice and compliance. The specific men and women who felt most threatened by the clergy women made deliberate efforts to privately and publicly undermine their pastoral leadership through judgement, control of a single narrative, aggression, and humiliation. This ongoing and often unchecked emotional projection led to acute and chronic psychological abuse, systemic scapegoating, and the eventual executive derailment of the clergy woman.

"Dissident Daughter": Unpacking the Mother-Daughter Wound

The women in this study noted intense interactions with specific women parishioners and/or denominational leaders, roughly ages 60–75, who were particularly critical of their pastoral leadership. As discussed earlier, the most vocal opponents seemed to harbor internalized sexism possibly resulting from patriarchal restrictions to their autonomy, choice, and voice within their own lived experiences. Certain women who exhibited this background may have perceived a more self-differentiated younger clergy woman as a threat to her own limited sense of agency and, as a result, actively participated in dismantling the clergy woman's leadership. The research participants consistently identified certain women in this demographic as targeting, bullying, and/or scapegoating in ways that severely undermined the clergy women's leadership.

The intergenerational conflict evident between certain older women and more self-differentiated women clergy reveals a pervasive "mother-daughter wound" within Protestant church culture. Hasseldine (2017) outlined this mother-daughter relational dynamic stating:

When the language that inquires after what women feel, think, and need is not spoken in a family, culture, and society, mothers and daughters are set up to fight over who gets to be heard. When emotional needs are ignored, mothers and daughters argue over whose needs get to be met in that relationship. (p.4)

The mother-daughter wound is prevalent in societies where younger women exercise significantly greater autonomy and self-differentiation than previous generations. In social contexts where there is less symmetry or mirroring between mothers and their adult daughters, older women may feel resentment, anger, and frustration. When examined further, older women who themselves have experienced gender oppression and have, as a result, absorbed certain gender role expectations, enter a kind of rivalry or competition with younger women who have greater social mobility (Hasseldine, 2017). The small close-knit nature of individual Protestant parishes has a striking resemblance to nuclear family structures where these intergenerational tensions are actively negotiated.

The resentment that certain older women parishioners project upon younger clergy women may be grounded in feelings of disappointment and lack of fulfillment in their own personal lives as well as prevailing gender expectations of the self-sacrificial woman within their own generational experience. This dynamic points to the "human giver syndrome," which Nagoski and Nagoski (2020) defined as the phenomenon whereby women, particularly those of childbearing age, continue to be expected to "give to humanity through their time, attention, affection, and bodies" (p.xiii). In social systems that perpetuate high expectations of gender-role congruency (Eagly & Karau, 2002), those who deviate from the gendered expectation of the female "human giver," such as self-differenced younger women clergy, experience social rejection and punishment.

Qualitative research on the mother-daughter relationship first took root in the field of psychology and early developments of relational cultural theory, in which empathy within the mother-daughter relationship served as an important counterpoint to long-standing developmental models that prioritized independent, self-oriented achievement (Jordan et al., 1991). However, this earlier research had the potential to idealize a compassionate mother-daughter bond and insufficiently addressed elements of intergenerational conflict between mothers and daughters. Stiver (1986) highlighted two co-existing realities in which the highly permeable boundaries between mothers and daughters contribute to girls and women developing more relational selves. At the same time, there is an ongoing cycle in which a mother may resent her daughter's process of self-individuation just as the daughter rejects the engulfing mother and her lack of differentiation (p.9). It is important to acknowledge the impact of surrounding patriarchal structures that limit female autonomy and agency and the ways in which those narratives are passed down between women. This form of generational trauma was a strong factor among certain older female parishioners' disapproval of younger more agentic women clergy.

Mother-daughter conflict is an historically under-researched dynamic due to societal shaming both within private familial relationships as well as in the fields of psychology and clinical counseling. Historical avoidance as well as the oversimplified accounts of Freud and Jung (Stiver, 1986), have prevented more nuanced exploration of the mother-daughter wound and its impact on family and workplace relationships. The systemic silencing and misrepresentation of this topic has been further complicated by public discourse that diagnoses female relational conflict as "women's own pathology, rather than the result of generational patriarchal patterns in family, culture, and society" (Hasseldine, 2017, p. xvii). The application of relational cultural theory, family systems theory, and social attachment theory has shed light on the more subconscious emotional landscapes that effect intergenerational female relationships. These areas of exploration are important to consider within the context of Protestant church culture and other related work environments where conflicting gender identity narratives, intergenerational conflict, and high levels of boundary permeability create a precarious leadership space for younger women leaders.

"Emasculating Disrupter": Destabilizing Narratives of Masculinity

The second typology of individuals who were most critical of the clergy women in this study were certain male clergy, church staff members, denominational leaders, and parishioners, who demonstrated rigid narratives of masculinity. The men that the women described represented a broader range of ages, roughly ages 40–75, as compared to the specifically Baby Boomer generation of women noted above. The clergy women identified the men's oppositional behaviors as being possibly rooted in social insecurities, for which the men may have been overcompensating by portraying higher levels of masculine authority and control.

There was a common feature in the interviews whereby a male

clergy or parishioner who was critical of the woman clergy had some kind of emotional instability in his personal life, such as a neglectful childhood or conflict in his personal relationships and/or marriage, which in some cases was magnified by addictive behaviors. These details were often readily known to the clergy woman, having worked closely with male clergy or parishioners in which these more private aspects of self were disclosed and directly communicated. There was also a professional and economic component, whereby a disaffected male parishioner with job insecurity, unemployment, or other financial struggles was more inclined to project emotions of distrust and anger toward a younger woman clergy who exhibited pastoral authority and healthy boundaries.

Cindy described a passive-aggressive male parishioner who reflected this profile through his use of threatening emails:

After I confronted him about these terrible emails, he said "I hope you won't be sharing this with anyone else." And I responded, "Yes, I am," and I copied the personnel committee in on that so fast saying, 'This is what he's been sending me for five years. This is the way that he talks to me. We need to stop this.' So, then he blew up, resigned from the church board, stomped off and said he would never be back and then kept showing up at church because he had keys to the building. He would show up at church when I was the only one there. And I never felt safe with him. He had a really violent temper. I had the building re-keyed and he showed up and couldn't get into the building and threw a huge temper tantrum. He spread around to all these people that I was trying to turn on him.

In terms of male clergy and denominational leaders, there was a display of toxic masculinity demonstrated through aggression, anger, and punishment of younger clergy women. This was particularly evident in the experiences shared by Sandra, Christine, and Vivienne, each of whom worked under older male senior pastors who exhibited extremely dehumanizing and psychologically abusive behaviors. Hope described an incident in which an older male clergy felt intimidated by her, was unsuccessful in belittling her, and ultimately transferred his feelings of emasculation onto another woman staff member:

> He finally said, "Well, you're right. I just have to admit you intimidate me." I said, "Well, that's a you problem, not a me problem." And we get done with him admitting that he's intimidated and he comes out of the office and goes to our new youth director. He starts telling her how she can do the children's sermon better. It was just this ridiculous thing and I went out and looked at him like, really? This is how you're choosing how to respond to me intimidating you? You're gonna try and intimidate the youth pastor so you can still feel like some big strong man? Or whatever was going on there. And he sees me staring at him like that and he just turns around and he walks away. And I looked at the youth director, and her eyes were just like, "What the heck was that?" I just said, "That wasn't about you. That was about me. So don't take any of that to heart."

This exchange points to possible overcompensation of feelings of insecurity, in which men who feel intimidated by a clergy women's agency and autonomy respond with efforts to degrade, humiliate, or otherwise silence their clergy women colleagues, particularly those who are associate pastors.

The application of social attachment theory offers great insight into the interiority of those who tend to reject clergy women and their expressions of agency and autonomy. Frost (2019) explained that attachment theory in family of origin systems and early caregiver relationships has a strong effect on relational conflict skills both in childhood and in adulthood. Those with histories of emotional neglect and unresolved relational trauma are likely to exhibit attachment deficiencies at various developmental stages, including poor conflict-resolution skills later in life. Such unmet emotional needs are often the very thing that draws individuals to seek affirmation and belonging within faith-based communities (Reiss, 2015).

Certain male parishioners, clergy, staff, and denominational leaders, who felt emasculated by intelligent, self-differentiated, well-respected younger clergy women, tended to adopt accusatory and scapegoating behaviors in order to uphold particular masculine narratives of control and authority. Such behavior may have been based on unmet emotional needs in early stages of human development. This is many ways mirrors the internalized sexism experienced by older women who were critical of younger clergy women. In both cases, individuals who felt their own agency was restricted in certain areas of their personal or professional life, were more likely to project their frustration over their own lack of self-actualization upon younger clergy women who confidently exhibited more autonomy.

Figure 4.5 illustrates the two profiles of individuals who exhibited the most resistance to the clergy women's leadership and overall personhood. While these profiles were consistently described throughout the interviews, it is important to acknowledge that this study did not capture the internal thought processes of the individuals themselves. Further discussion on why these individuals may have been more prone to target younger agentic clergy women will be discussed in the following chapter on gendered scapegoating and mimetic rivalry.

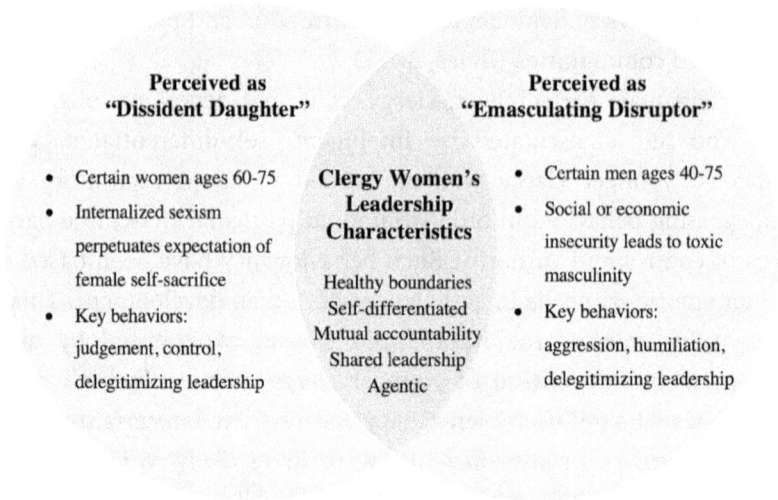

Perceived as "Dissident Daughter"	Clergy Women's Leadership Characteristics	Perceived as "Emasculating Disruptor"
• Certain women ages 60-75 • Internalized sexism perpetuates expectation of female self-sacrifice • Key behaviors: judgement, control, delegitimizing leadership	Healthy boundaries Self-differentiated Mutual accountability Shared leadership Agentic	• Certain men ages 40-75 • Social or economic insecurity leads to toxic masculinity • Key behaviors: aggression, humiliation, delegitimizing leadership

Copyright 2024 by Lynn M. Horan

Figure 4.5: Perceptions of Gen-X/Millennial Clergy Women as a "Dissident Daughter" and an "Emasculating Disruptor"

While the women in this study did not seek to be intentionally disruptive, their very existence and desire to lead in collaborative and agentic ways activated feelings of resistance among individuals with more rigid gender identity narratives. As a result, negative perceptions regarding the identity and leadership practices of the clergy women in this study, led to a highly unstable social system that delegitimized and ultimately derailed the clergy women, despite their otherwise effective and well-respected leadership and relational practices.

5

DISMANTLED

As the clergy women continued to negotiate the realities of feminized servanthood and engage in intentional efforts to differentiate themselves within unhealthy congregations, when system anxiety intensified there were key moments in which the clergy women identified toxic leadership around them and persistent institutional gaslighting. These combined realities resulted in a persistent scapegoating mechanism against more self-differentiated clergy women, a dynamic that is addressed in detail below through the lens of René Girard's (1966, 1977, 1986, 1987) theory of mimetic rivalry. These experiences are described in the following categories of *exposing toxic leaders and harmful systems, nail in the coffin* and *becoming the target.*

EXPOSING TOXIC LEADERS AND HARMFUL SYSTEMS

The category of *exposing vs. protecting toxic leaders and harmful systems* included significant sharing around the clergy women's own efforts to promote transparency and shared accountability within their ministry contexts. The interviews revealed a combined process of 1) the clergy women exposing problematic elements by promoting transparency, accountability, and equitability, which was then met with 2) individuals, congregations, and larger denominational structures protecting problematic elements in the form of deliberate silencing, overt dismissiveness, and gaslighting. These dynamics were reflected in the social processes of *dealing with toxic leaders, your voice has no reality,* and *no one taking a stand* (see Table 5.1).

Primary Dimension	Conceptual Categories and Corresponding Social Processes		
Exposing vs. Protecting Toxic Leaders and Harmful Systems	**Dealing With Toxic Leaders** • Toxic masculinity and throwing weight around • Internalized sexism • Others controlling/ manipulating the narrative	**Your Voice Has No Reality** • Gaslighting • Vortex of insanity • Thrown under the bus	**No One Taking a Stand** • Fed to the wolves • Dismissing sexual misconduct • Moral disalignment

Table 5.1: Primary Dimension: Exposing vs. Protecting Toxic Leaders and Harmful Systems

Dealing with Toxic Leaders

Within the social process of *dealing with toxic leaders,* the women utilized a variety of leadership strengths, emotional intelligence, and coping mechanisms in order to negotiate extremely difficult working relationships. As the relational dynamics became untenable, and in many cases abusive, the women shared what it felt like to expose the unhealthy and dysfunctional elements within their ministry contexts. The women often faced concrete efforts on the part of others to protect particular leaders and harmful systems of church culture and governance. The women experienced toxic leaders, both men and women, at every level of the church system, including local congregations, church boards and staff, and denominational leadership.

Toxic leaders represented a variety of identities including gender, race, age, and sexual orientation. As noted earlier, the primary typologies that emerged were 1) insecure men of various ages wanting to reinforce certain narratives of masculinity and 2) older women with internalized sexism who imposed rigid gender expectations on younger clergy women. A third typology also emerged whereby congregations were unwilling to hold toxic leaders accountable in part because of a pastor's marginalized identity. This was evident with an older White lesbian pastor within a very pro-LGBTQ denomination and a Black male pastor in a predominantly White denomination engaged in racial justice work. In both of these ministry contexts, the research participants noted that while the surrounding church system acknowledged each of the leaders' toxic behaviors, they seemed unwilling to hold them accountable because of a marginalized identity.

Toxic Masculinity and Throwing Weight Around

A common form of harmful leadership that the women encountered was toxic masculinity, which Sandra defined as:

Masculinity is just the fact of being male and identifying as male and how do you embody that. I would say that toxic masculinity is using your maleness to exert power and control over people and situations where the system has historically been in your favor. And you are exploiting that to gain more power and to oppress other people in some way.

Marta observed similar behaviors of toxic masculinity from a psychologically abusive senior pastor. She observed the male senior pastor acting out more aggressively when he felt threatened by women with a strong sense of self who were not easily manipulated:

What has been the problem with my heads of staff is both of them I think are threatened by strong women. I have a very strong personality. I'm ready to call BS when I can do it. At my last congregation, a woman who took the position that I vacated was a colleague of mine. I feel like she doesn't have as strong of a personality and she's someone who can be easily manipulated and walked all over and she'll just take it. She has been at that call as long as I've been at my current one. She is still there under him. Another clergy friend of mine who came on staff overlapped with me for a few months. She also had a very strong personality. She didn't last two years and had all the same complaints that I did.

Vivienne described toxic masculinity as a form of insecurity in which the senior pastor would humiliate her to make himself feel more powerful:

The previous male senior pastor I worked with really modeled how to lead with integrity, so it was disorienting for me to be sitting around a table where I would say something and people would roll their eyes at me or shut down what I was saying or asking. There were times when the senior pastor really treated me like I was dumb. Which was so bizarre. I mean, I think to be honest, I don't think he was that smart. I don't think he had the capacity to keep up with us intellectually or just in general. And I think he didn't like that and didn't like to be challenged, so he surrounded himself with other men who would just pat him on the back, whatever he said. And then to sit around a table where there was just nonsense happening and then to be treated as if I was dumb and not bright enough to figure out what was going on.

Several women noted toxic masculinity being expressed in controlling or punitive ways that silenced any form of dialogue or discussion. Sandra continually observed a male senior pastor "throwing his weight around in unhealthy ways and not being willing to dialogue." Marta noted similar behaviors of physical intimidation, isolation, and punishment, noting:

The senior pastor's office became a place of trauma because of the meeting that happened there. Whenever he said, "Can I see you in my office?" all the staff members felt traumatized because whenever we were called into his office, we were yelled at or we were punished.

Internalized Sexism

In addition to the abuses of power exhibited by male senior pastors, there were numerous instances of toxic leadership from older women, including other clergy, church members, and staff. Unlike toxic male leaders who were both similar ages to the women clergy as well as older, toxic leadership among women came in the form of internalized sexism from women predominantly in the age range of 60–75.

Haley described an older female senior pastor as needing a "pressure release gate" and was invested in Haley's "wrongness":

I did set boundaries when she would blow up. And it was clear to me that we're not going anywhere right then. I would say, "Okay, I see this is going on and I don't think that we can resolve this effectively right now. Let's come back to it in our weekly scheduled meeting time." And then when that would happen, she would just get activated again. I tried to give her the benefit of the doubt, validate her perception of the interaction and say, "I understand why that would be frustrating" and gently share what I was experiencing and recognize that there was a difference there and propose ways of moving forward.

She was never willing to see my side of it, the way that I was willing to see hers. She wasn't willing to admit any wrongdoing. She only wanted to sort of berate me. I felt like I was this pressure release gate for her. She needed someone to bait and for someone to be wrong. She was so invested in my wrongness and her need for rightness to be affirmed. Her need for my difference of some kind. I don't know, but she could not, we couldn't, compromise.

Christy, who was an associate pastor working under co-pastors who were married, noted feeling like she was the "triangulator" between the toxic and passive-aggressive leadership of both pastors:

> They had been at the church for 22 years. And it became really evident to me the longer I served in ministry there that they had really bad communication with the congregation. The woman had severe conflicts with multiple people in the congregation and those had been brought to the other pastor, which is her spouse. But he did not address them and so when I came in as a third pastor, I just got this flood of responses from congregation members saying "We won't serve on this committee with her" or "This is the way she pushed me out of ministry" or "This is why I don't go on Sunday mornings anymore." And so, I kind of became the triangulator, because I think for literally decades people had been trying to tell the [male] pastor we have conflict with the [female] pastor but because of the nature of their relationship that was not listened to.

Others Controlling and Manipulating the Narrative

While unhealthy leadership behaviors were exhibited differently through the toxic masculinity of certain men and the internalized sexism of older women, both men and women utilized the common tactic of *controlling and manipulating the narrative*. This was often evident during formal annual staff reviews, in which other clergy or church leaders would directly reject the perspectives of the clergy woman. In addition, there was misrepresentation of broader communal narratives related to church administration and congregational approaches to social justice. Vivienne described the process of others' "twisting my words" in ways that were inaccurate and manipulative:

> The senior pastor would take something you said or rightly asked for, like a day off or to be more with your family, which

was my big thing, and they would start to twist those words into a narrative that was really unfair. And it was really odd to watch it happen because someone would come on staff and there'd be such a fanfare. And they would be like, this person is going to remake X and it would go along swimmingly until it didn't. And then that switch. You couldn't figure out what happened. We were all sitting around the same table. And we could never understand what happened. And the senior pastor would just say, "Oh well, they're not coming to this meeting. Oh, well, they're not doing this. They won't be present at that." And it was just this complete change of narrative.

LaVerne described manipulation in the form of financial misconduct and "wheeling and dealing" at both the congregational and denominational levels, which she could no longer tolerate:

It often happened when we were counting money, which is a very intriguing thing. When the people who typically count money—usually men—weren't around, and they'd have to call a woman to do it and they would absolutely hate to have to do that, particularly me, because I know how to count numbers and I would not let them lie or write the wrong numbers or take out money or anything like that.

Christy described a staff review meeting in which she was presented with a lengthy document that accused her of "coercion, manipulation, and threats." She was specifically accused of reorganizing the church library "without any authority," which Christy used as an opportunity to share how she had experienced the incident much differently:

The library director asked if I could help go through a bunch of donated books on theology and sexuality, to make sure there wasn't anything homophobic. So, I went and spent four hours with her and another volunteer and I got to know them and dusted and stuff. I had a great time. It was one of the first space things that I helped to improve because I think the use of church space is really important. It's a way of being theologically open. And we made a pile of books to donate and we asked the male pastor, "Here's the pile, will you please review them before we get rid of them?" So, none of it was done on my own volition. None of it was self-initiated by me. It was a great relational experience and all of it was done in community. It was meant to make our library more affirming and it was done in consultation with the male pastor. As I said that during my staff review meeting, he was like, "Yeah, I guess you did ask me to do that."

Joan described the senior pastor of her congregation controlling the narrative regarding the congregation's affirmation of the LGBTQ+ community:

He had created a narrative that the people who went to his church were outsiders and wouldn't fit in anywhere else and nobody else would take them and they were the only true safe church for people who had affirming theologies. Which again is not true because we also were one of the only affirming churches who didn't have a queer person on staff. But everybody really bought into this narrative that if their church died, they had nowhere to go.

Christy felt that her desire to promote an inclusive approach to leadership that drew upon a co-created communal narrative, was perceived as threatening and unwelcome by her supervising female pastor:

I think she cannot be in a leadership position if she doesn't feel in control of the narrative. It's not actually based on a specific ethic around an issue either. I think that when she feels she's not in control of something, then she wants to just reject it. So, if she's not in control of the meeting I do not think she has the openness or capacity to learn new things. And that is not a good thing to be as a leader.

Allegra noted, "There was a story of 'Oh yeah, Allegra's doing great. She's so wonderful,' that was fed to folks out in the pews. But behind the scenes it was an about face." Rose felt similar noting:

I was at a very historic church and embraced by a very large community outside the walls of the church. And everything seems so great, but behind the scenes I witnessed some very disheartening processes and behaviors that just were not in alignment with what I believed God was calling me to.

Your Voice Has No Reality

Gaslighting

Controlling the narrative was also evident in the form of gaslighting, in which the clergy women were made to feel that their experience, perspective, or description of certain dynamics, concerns, or incidents were not valid or real. Deborah was told by a denominational leader, "Your voice has no reality," after she raised concern that social media content she had shared had been used in a denominational presentation as a way to illustrate why congregations were leaving the denomination. Deborah felt she was constantly under surveillance, noting that:

A single tweet about a feeling produced this firestorm of resistance and hatred. I was being surveilled and the point of their work was to get me to shut up, like they didn't want my voice. A denominational leader told me once that my voice had no

145

reality. Literally, word for word, "Your voice has no reality in this conversation."

Hope described gaslighting and intense feelings of betrayal that came with being a leader who promoted transparency and mutual accountability within a dysfunctional system that ultimately sought only to protect itself:

> I look at the system in terms of it being narcissistic. It makes you feel like it's this safe space, with all these colleagues that are all in the same boat together and we all have some of these similar struggles. But then the moment that you raise a red flag about something and it happens to be about somebody that they are, for whatever reason, invested in protecting, or maybe friends with, suddenly you're a "persona non grata," and they do what they can to really wear you down and make you question your own reality. You start to think, is it really as bad as I think it is? Maybe it's not. Maybe this is normal. Maybe this is how it's supposed to be. It was such a disorienting feeling.

Marta noted that having two retired clergy in the congregation, a woman and a man, validated her observations of being gaslit, which helped her to stay grounded:

> I love these people dearly. They are so grounded. They are so healthy and hold confidence so well. I am able to go to them and say, "Here's what the senior pastor said. Here's what I think of the situation that's going on. Am I being gaslit? Am I being manipulated? Or is there something to what they're saying?" And about 99% of the time, they say, "No, he's wrong. Yeah, you've got a good head on your shoulders." Having that person to ground me and to be able to say, "This is right. This is wrong. Your inclination that you're being manipulated is correct. Keep doing what you're doing," that has prob-

ably saved me and kept me at my current call longer than I would have.

Sandra described being silenced and gaslit during her resignation, in which church leaders pressured her to not disclose what actually happened:

> I was told it was inappropriate for me to tell the congregation that the board had asked for my resignation and the board members literally said, "We didn't ask you to resign." I had the letter in my hand where the board asked for my resignation. The blatant gaslighting was so overwhelming. That evening I no longer had access to my church email account. I was told that I was being put on paid leave for the last month and I wasn't allowed back in the building.

Vortex of Insanity

Hope entered her ministry context as an associate pastor, having been given no information about the current senior pastor's sexual misconduct with the previous female associate pastor. She shared that the gaslighting and silencing around the misconduct felt like "a vortex of insanity," noting:

> Gaslighting is when people make you question your own experiences and your own reality. People start with, "Did that really happen? Is that really the way it went?" Or they just flat out lie and say it was something else that went down. It felt like I was right back in this weird vortex of insanity again and thinking, what is this and how is this ever allowed to continue on?

Joanna, a solo pastor and head-of-staff, described her struggle to cope with a verbally abusive staff member, who eventually became intolerable:

Over the course of five and a half years I tried to respond to her behavior pastorally and with some empathy. But there were a couple times where I got verbally sliced pretty significantly by her. She would go on long rants and she would talk without taking a break and she would throw accusations in all along the way. It was just insane. Eventually, to cope with it I just set a timer. And that way I could pay attention to the timer.

Thrown Under the Bus

Several women identified instances when they or other women staff members attempted to be transparent about congregational dynamics, which led to denial and defensive behaviors on the part of other church leadership. The feeling of being "thrown under the bus" spoke to the highly protective measures of toxic leaders who sought to maintain their positions of authority at all costs. Joan described a senior pastor who asked her to intervene in a certain congregational conflict, only to deny any conflict when it was brought to others' attention:

I would get into a group meeting and I would say, "Hey, it's come to my attention that there seems to be some things going on here. Can we talk about that?" And everybody would get upset and the senior pastor would go, "Joan, what are you talking about?" and literally throw me under the bus.

Or I would approach him privately about something that I thought was concerning with child safety or with uses of finances. And then in meetings, he would bring up things to try to undermine me and say, "I know that Joan is concerned about this but obviously we would never think that about this person." Things that should have been handled in confidence that were instead used to turn the community against me.

Marta described a female staff member "being thrown under the bus" by the male senior pastor because she exposed ways in which he had lied about her to other staff:

> He was telling things about her to staff members behind her back. Staff members told her, and she confronted him about it and he lied to her about having done it. She caught him in that lie and she's now leaving the church. It was lies on top of lies. He will throw his staff under a bus before making himself look bad. You know, we're all expendable, but he's like the Almighty God in the church.

No One Taking a Stand

The category of *no one taking a stand* represents the overall lack of accountability, including church boards not holding other clergy accountable for mistreatment of other staff, regional boards not holding congregations accountable for misrepresenting their ability to hire a full-time pastor, and denominational governance not holding clergy accountable for mismanagement of funds and sexual misconduct. These unstable elements created a reality in which the clergy women were placed in precarious calls that compromised their overall physical and psychological safety, financial security, and emotional well-being. These dynamics were reflected in the social processes of *fed to the wolves, dismissing sexual misconduct,* and *moral disalignment.*

Fed to the Wolves

Hope described the experience of being placed in a highly precarious call in which she was not informed of the senior pastor's recent history of sexual misconduct. After raising concerns to multiple individuals within the denominational system, her voice was continually silenced or minimized:

> It was so disheartening to feel like they had fed me to the wolves. And then, when I came screaming, "There are wolves,"

they were like, "Are you sure? Are you sure there are wolves? We don't think there are wolves." I think that's the part that really gets to me. There are so many parts that get to me, but it's just the fact that they knew this about him. And they still sent me in there. And sent me in saying, "Well, if you see anything" and when I said, "Okay, I'm seeing something," to still have let it go down the way it did.

Allegra, who was verbally attacked by a well-known male clergy known for his social justice work in the denomination, felt that those who were loyal to him made excuses for his behavior:

Fortunately, I had enough fortitude afterwards to go and talk to some other people about it and they did follow up with it. But it didn't feel very satisfying because they were like, "Well, you know, he's been sick." Then why was he at the meeting if he's sick? I've been sick and I don't treat people like shit.

Several women noted that they were hired by congregations that were dishonest or not forthcoming about their ability to offer a fair salary as outlined in their contracts. Kay observed that the lack of transparency around the church's finances prior to her arrival caused her to be blamed for not having "figured out the finances of the church":

There was one woman in particular that in hindsight had way too much power, but she was already in those positions when I came in. She was the chair of the administrative council and chair of the finance committee and so had a lot of power and she was the one who just kept landing on me hard for not figuring out the finances of this church. To this day, I do not know if the push for a full-time clergy person after years and years of having somebody part-time came from the church or came from the denomination. My saving grace was that I had already seen the writing on the wall. I had done the math.

Deborah, who was very open about her commitments to LGBTQ+ inclusivity, requested protection for herself during a denominational meeting based on a previous death threat within the denomination:

> Right before the denominational meeting I asked my supervisors, "These people are very angry with me and they have a documented history of violence. What protections are available for me?" I didn't want to be in an enclosed space. People knew who I was, where I was, and had been very angry at me. Death threats were put under the hotel room door of a lesbian leader in the church at our annual conference. So, it wasn't an unfounded concern to ask for protection. But there was none. Absolutely nothing was done about it that.

While there was no concrete response to her request for protection, Deborah acknowledged that her ability to ask for protection was more than what was afforded her denominational colleagues who are clergy Women of Color:

> I was terrified. But there's the other side of that coin in that I'm a pretty privileged White woman and so I have a sense of being protected. My Women of Color friends in the denomination have told me that is very different than how they feel.

Dismissing Sexual Misconduct

In one of the most disturbing moments of sharing, LaVerne described both men and women minimizing and silencing ongoing sexual misconduct between male denominational leaders and young women seeking ordination:

> There was a culture of sexual misconduct. Even after a denomination leader who was a woman addressed the behaviors, it didn't necessarily stop with her, it just went underground. There were power dynamic issues, not as much with me, but I

had to step in for a lot of my younger female colleagues. One or two got pregnant by male pastors that were on the ordination board. One had an abortion; one had the baby. But you know, that was just kind of the culture in that particular area. It pissed me off particularly when it was towards women seeking ordination.

I remember being in a meeting where a male pastor was required to sit down for six months, and I was sitting next to another woman who was a clergy and she said, "I don't know why he has to do that. If God forgives him, surely we can." And I just looked at her like she had lost her mind. How are you making sexual misconduct towards someone okay? We tried to encourage the women to speak up if something happened, particularly the students. But it was a power thing you know, if this person of power that's on the ordination board can make or break you being ordained. They didn't feel they had a voice.

Sandra's denomination arranged for a counselor to meet with her and her male senior pastor, who had a known cocaine addiction and ongoing sexual relationships with other staff and church members. The counselor, who was a colleague of the senior pastor, dismissed and minimized the reports of sexual misconduct:

When I came to the counselor and I said "I feel like Gary is keeping inappropriate boundaries with a church staff member," the counselor just said, "People have different understandings of boundaries." That's not the right answer. I mean, as a counselor he should have said, "What do you mean by that?" and asked me for more information to clarify. Instead, he just dismissed my concern out of hand and it turns out that yes, Gary was indeed violating every boundary in the book.

Hope, who described her experience earlier as being "fed to the wolves," found that the senior pastor's misconduct with youth and other staff members was enabled on multiple occasions:

At the time, I don't know that I was trying to challenge the system as a whole. I was trying to do what I thought I was supposed to be doing. I thought it was my responsibility to report this stuff. And to say, hey maybe this needs to be looked at and investigated further because I've got a youth director here who's telling me that the senior pastor is making really inappropriate sexual comments about minors. That's not something you just brush off and laugh about. There were so many red flags.

Moral Disalignment

The women described feeling that they were in a kind "altered universe," in which the surrounding social system operated along a different set of ethics, social norms, and rules of engagement. Within the category of *moral disalignment,* there was a feeling of existing in two worlds, which became further intensified when the women promoted transparency and mutual accountability surrounding issues of financial or sexual misconduct, or exposed instances of toxic leadership.

Rose, a Black clergy woman, described the "double consciousness" or "twoness" that she faced working within in a predominantly Black denomination, where she struggled to navigate the space of Black communal identity within a larger White or Western narrative:

Similar to what W. E. B Du Bois calls this "twoness," where we're Black and from the African diaspora being introduced forcefully into a nation that was predominantly White. We have to show up in both systems in order to seek liberation for ourselves. We couldn't do so just one sided. We have to learn the other side as well and I felt like I've done that for ten years. I was involved in pastoral leadership where I would work with people that were choosing this capitalistic Western way of thinking and having power over people. That's where ego comes in. You're so stuck in your ego and stuck in this Western way of thinking that you have totally forgotten about the

African traditional religions and midnight hush harbors when we were enslaved.

The double consciousness described by Rose pointed to her particular racialized experience as a Black clergy woman working in an historically Black denomination. This experience was not mirrored by the White clergy women, due to their position of racial privilege and affiliation with White denominations. However, the White clergy women did experience a form of moral-misalignment, or cognitive dissonance, in which they felt compelled to go along with a dehumanizing and dysfunctional system out of a need for financial and employment security, or simply because they didn't realize how bad the dynamics were. Vivienne noted:

There were a lot of things happening around that table, some of which I was not privy to because I was not in the boys' club. Some of which I sensed was happening and couldn't parse out. And maybe some of which I felt I was even silent toward at some point and I didn't realize how nefarious it was until it was too late.

NAIL IN THE COFFIN AND BECOMING THE TARGET

Over time, the exposure to unhealthy, toxic, and abusive social dynamics, severely compromised the women's psychological safety and physical health. All of the women had experiences of realizing when they had had enough, which many described as the "nail in the coffin" or the "final straw." This feeling often solidified after growing awareness that the clergy women were being targeted or sabotaged in some way within their ministry contexts. As the levels of dysfunctionality intensified, some of the women felt they had more agency and ability to advocate for themselves, while others felt increasingly silenced and isolated. Whether one felt pushed out, forced to leave, or was able to leave on one's own terms, each of the women recalled important decisions they made around their work, personal lives, and physical safety. These dynamics are outlined through the following social processes of *becoming the target, life was threatened,* and *deciding to leave.*

Primary Dimension	Conceptual Categories and Corresponding Social Processes		
	Becoming the Target	Life was Threatened	Deciding to Leave
Nail in the Coffin	• Lightening rod	• Not seen as human	• Vulnerability in betrayal
	• Scapegoating	• Body taking me out	• Throwing my hands up
	• Ousting the threat	• Staying will kill you	• Saving my life

Table 5.2: Primary Dimension: Nail in the Coffin

Becoming the Target

The category of *becoming the target* was experienced by almost all of the women and was described with incredibly powerful language and imagery. The depth and enormity of the specific experiences are divided into three chronological processes of *lightening rod, scapegoating,* and *ousting the threat.* Figures 5.1, 5.2, and 5.3 illustrate the verbatim language used by the women to describe each of these social processes.

Lightning Rod

The social process of the *lightning rod* speaks to the building momentum of negative perception and criticism around the clergy women. Derived from family systems theory, the "lightning rod effect" points to the phenomenon whereby relatively self-differentiated individuals within a social system become a focal point for system anxiety and ultimately absorb or become the target for others' unresolved conflict (Jalovec et al., 2011). For the clergy women in this study, this process often developed over time and would escalate during times of leadership transition, conflicts around important decisions within the church and/or surrounding community, polarization around national politics and issues of social justice, as well as expressions of self-differentiation on the part of the clergy woman.

Dragged along into it	Wrapped up into	Anxiety spiral
Triangulating	Going downhill	Firestorm of resistance
Grouped together against	Swept up	Corralling around

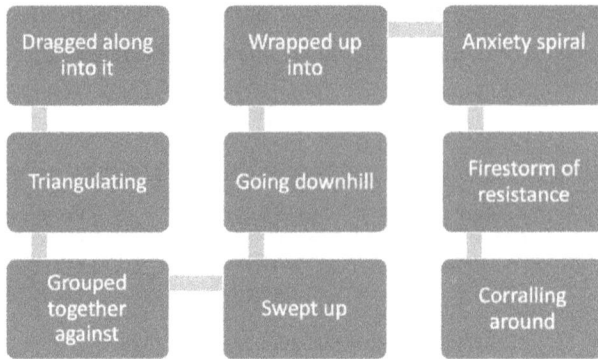

Figure 5.1: Interview Language Related to Lightning Rod

Allegra had significant training in family systems theory as part of her seminary education and described the lightning rod effect in the following way:

When somebody differentiates away from the system, in response, the system fights back by making that person or situation the identified patient. They become the problem. And in doing that it's like lightning. Lightning hits where there's metal, or there's something to attract it. So, the system is electrically charged up with this feeling that they've done something one way all the time. And then by just physically being there as a human being and the first female pastor, I became a lightning rod for all this electrical energy about feelings about politics. I was an easy target for all the anxiety they'd been storing up.

Kay described a similar phenomenon of an "anxiety spiral," which she experienced from a group of mothers in the congregation where she served as the director of youth and families:

I generally had a pretty positive experience until this time when three moms of kids in my program got themselves into an anxiety spiral and looking back, I think it was tied to power. They were three of the parents who had really advocated for my position to be established, but they also had the most leadership in that area prior to me being hired. When I came in, I think they felt a loss of power and control over the program. The head pastor was also new, so I also think it was a little bit of a lightning rod sort of phenomenon, maybe within that pastoral change. They couldn't be mad at the lead pastor, so they'd be mad at me. So, I left there on not great terms.

Scapegoating

The social processes of the lightning rod and scapegoating are intricately related, with the initial stage of the lightening rod representing the growing anxiety within the system being directed at the clergy women, often without conscious awareness on the part of the clergy woman's opponents. This then led to a scapegoating dynamic, in which individuals would "bond together" or "group together" against" the clergy women through often ungrounded accusations that were spread throughout the community. Individuals would become "swept up," "spooled around," or "wrapped up into it," in ways that left the clergy women unable to defend or protect themselves within the system (see Figure 5.2).

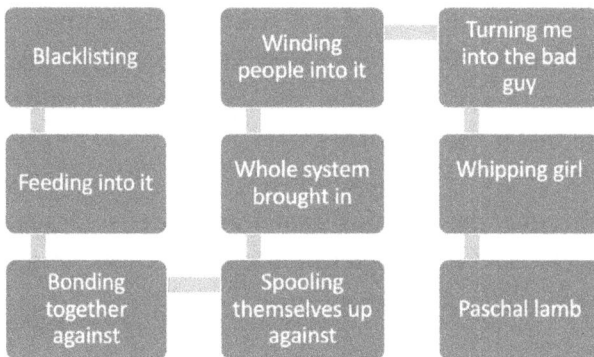

Figure 5.2: Interview Language Related to Scapegoating

Sandra described the process of scapegoating while working with a charismatic male co-pastor who had a history of drug addiction and sexual misconduct within the congregation:

> The concept of scapegoating is that the responsible person has no consequences for their actions and that all of it gets passed off on to another person. That was what happened when Gary finally resigned from his call, all of the reasons for it somehow became my fault. I was the only staff member left and he had told the church leaders it was my fault. Without him being present to discuss it further, they just took his message word for word, and put all the blame and burden of his misconduct on to me. All of a sudden, these people who I thought that I knew and who I thought trusted me, were accusing me of things that I had never done.

Joanna oversaw a church board and several staff members who eventually "bonded together against" her following her efforts to clarify job descriptions and structures of accountability:

> They constantly were spooling themselves up against this. So, I just kept putting in more and more boundaries around the staff, because the church itself had amazing ministry. The staff bonded together against me, went to the personnel committee, wrote a letter indicating that I wasn't collaborative, or they didn't feel supported in their work, and comments that I was "clearly unhappy." They told the personnel committee they really needed to "deal with me."

Hope described how confusing it was to feel scapegoated as she felt both herself and the congregation created "cover stories" that did not reflect the reality of her experience:

> The problem with telling cover stories when you're being scapegoated, is that you get so good at telling cover stories you

forget the real reason you're leaving, to the point that you default to the cover story without even thinking about it until after the fact.

A spiritual director who worked with Elsa used the term "whipping girl," a term that Elsa resisted at the time, but ultimately agreed with, as it reflected the kind of aggressive targeting that she experienced:

I worked with a spiritual director for years who saw lots of other female clergy and she said "Every woman pastor I know from this denomination is treated like a 'whipping girl.' She is being harmed intentionally by her congregation and by the larger system." And I struggle with that and yet I believe it. Young clergy women are seen as a whipping girl for the congregation. Everyone's anxiety about church growth, about decline, about a legacy, about, even the inherent punishment or shame dynamics within their faith narrative, is taken out on women. Men are elevated and exalted. Women are the paschal lambs.

Ousting the Threat

Following the lightning rod effect and the scapegoating phenomenon, a third social process of *ousting the threat* involved removing the clergy woman from her leadership position, either by making the woman's experience so physically and/or psychologically intolerable that she ultimately resigned, or an employment contract was not renewed. The ousting process often escalated when the clergy woman was on leave either for maternity leave, medical leave, or study leave, in which she was not present to defend or advocate for herself.

A common trend was also the practice of behind-the-scenes letter writing campaigns typically by other women, and occasionally by men, which served to build dissent and suspicion against the clergy woman within the larger church community or denomination. The final efforts to "get rid" of the clergy woman are illustrated by powerful verbatim language noted in Figure 5.3.

Figure 5.3: Interview Language Related to Ousting the Threat

Joan became a target in her ministry setting after she was hospitalized due to a known environmental hazard in the church building. She later voiced the need to address the issue in order to promote safety for others in the building:

> To me, it felt like I was trying to express a hurt and a concern for the health of the community, and it was immediately received as a legal threat. I felt like I was trying to have a conversation with a group of people I was supposed to be doing life with. And instead, all they could hear was, "What if she sues us? We can't have this. This can't be. This can't be a thing." But I never brought that up. I never even said the word "illegal." Although I should have. It felt like I immediately became the threat to their community and their community's existence. And something that was making their community bad. And they had to oust me in order to keep going.

Kay described the process of being pushed out of her ministry context after being hospitalized for a stress-induced illness:

Things spiraled, I got sick and was hospitalized. One of church members visited me in the hospital and said, "It would be so sad if our church was known as a church that chewed up and spit out a young clergy woman. We don't want to be known that way." The last week I was at the church, three people on the board were saying things to me that I thought, "This isn't you." People who had been allies suddenly turned on me. And then within two weeks the head of the board said, "We're gonna ask you to leave," which you can't do in my denomination, but a day later, a denominational representative called me and said, "They're really done with you."

Jenny felt that after a period of time, the congregation no longer had "confidence in me as a leader," and no longer supported her ministry work:

I think it was ultimately a desire to have control and trying to just keep me in the pulpit, just stay there, right? Some people loved my preaching, and those were the people who were very supportive. But in the end, I'm not even sure people really loved my worship leadership or my preaching. They were just sick of me.

Marta, who had been verbally attacked by a male senior pastor and a group of female church members, learned that she had been reported to a denominational leader:

There was a mandatory meeting that I had to attend with these angry women in the senior pastor's office at 10:00 a.m. on Wednesday. And this is when I learned that apparently whatever I did was so heinous that he had to call the denominational representative to say he "didn't know what to do with me."

Hope, who had dealt with significant gaslighting and minimizing of the senior pastor's sexual misconduct, felt ousted in the form of being placed in an adjacent church instead of directly dealing with her concerns over physical safety:

> A large part of why I left was I got sidelined to our second site because the senior pastor refused to deal with the danger posed by an unstable church member and refused to take seriously my concerns not just for my safety, but the safety of the congregation. A board member texted me saying, "You need to watch your back, she's gunning for you," because the church member was ranting on social media about how awful I was. Finally, the board president said he didn't think there was an "overt threat" being made, but what did I want done? I said I wanted a no-trespass order. Instead, I was sent away.

Joanna, a solo pastor and head of staff who underwent trauma therapy after leaving her ministry context, described being ousted as a form of "strategic sabotage":

> After I left, these kinds of flashbacks happened. And what I realized was there really was a pattern of the female music director trying to sabotage me emotionally. She was trying to push me toward some sort of public breakdown. It was less about her own anxiety but a strategic sabotage to attempt that. After I left, I wrote down all those conversations during trauma therapy, one by one. I just kind of worked through the emotion so that I could store those as memories instead of still feeling them in the present moment.

A few women described letter-writing campaigns that were initiated by a small group of disaffected congregants, and later sent to denominational leaders in an effort to remove the clergy woman. Cindy, a solo pastor, described what it felt like to learn that such tactics had been deployed before she even started the job:

Starting to dig through this, I realized that a member of the church had started writing letters to the denominational offices, some six years prior, personally attacking me before I was installed. So, I discovered that had started years ago, basically when I walked in the door. He decided he didn't like my style and had been personally attacking me for years. He had said all sorts of things to all kinds of people in the church who claimed to support me, and none of them had ever told him he needed to stop. None of them had ever spoken to me about it. None of them had ever intervened in any way and I had no idea.

The further I dug into things the more layers of just years of people sabotaging me behind my back. While I was thinking we were having really fruitful ministry and doing really exciting things together, there was a whole segment of the congregation who was just running everything down.

Life was Threatened

The category of *life was threatened* revealed dangerous levels of physical and/or psychological abuse that became life-threatening, including suicidal ideation, physical incapacitation, hospitalization, death threats, and the stress-induced deaths of ministry colleagues. Such extreme threats to life ultimately caused some of the women to question prior feelings of "sacrificial embrace" (Greene & Robbins, 2015), which previously had caused them to override or tolerate abusive conditions due to their strong sense of purpose or calling. The social processes of *not seen as human, body taking me out,* and *staying will kill you* are described below and refer to the extreme levels of dehumanization that ultimately caused the clergy women to leave toxic ministry contexts.

Not Seen as Human

For many of the women, there was a feeling of not being allowed to be human. This was exhibited in earlier discussions, when the women felt they were not able to express a range of human emotions, or live in a human body that has limitations. Melanie's experience being pregnant and having two children while working as a solo pastor alerted her to the extreme denial of her humanity. She asked herself the question, "Can I be a person that is a person with a body that does normal body things? Not all of those need to matter to people in the pews."

Several women noted physical and mental health conditions that necessitated medical leave, which was well within denominational policy. The women often had to navigate ongoing negotiations in order to justify their requests, with some ultimately being denied leave when it was desperately needed. During an extremely stressful time following a natural disaster, Cora became suicidal and was denied requests for medical leave, which ultimately informed her decision to leave active ministry:

I was doing disaster relief coordination. The denomination was sending work teams and supplies from all over the state. And I was facilitating that and it was killing me. One of the reasons they gave for denying medical leave was that because I had not been hospitalized or had not attempted suicide, they didn't think it was serious enough. But in the paperwork, if I had done that, I would not have been eligible to receive the support. It was really the most insane thing.

This institution has no capacity to care about people, because it wouldn't have even taken that much support to be okay. It was the worst experience of my life. Even after they granted the medical leave, after I got the financial support, the kinds of conversations I would have to have. I mean, it was so obvious that they just gave me the money because I was persistent. They never believed that I deserved it.

Jenny described the heartbreaking experience of having had a stillbirth and feeling pressured to return after only two weeks of bereavement:

I was pregnant and the baby died halfway through the pregnancy. So, I gave birth to the baby and then we had the baby cremated. We went to our home state to have the ashes buried and, along the way, the pastor would call me occasionally and ask when I was coming back. I just said, "I can't come back yet." I was completely traumatized from this, utterly traumatized. And I couldn't think about anything else except simply surviving. Once two weeks elapsed from when I was in the hospital to give birth, they sent me a check and had terminated my position at the church.

Sarah described the inability of others to see her as a "human who hurts," both during the intensity of two death threats she endured and afterward during her recovery:

They thought of me only as a helper and not one of the primary victims. As a pastor you're not seen as a human who hurts. And when I resigned, I still ran into people and they're like, "I still remember your last sermon about the Japanese art form of filling broken pottery with gold." And they thought that was so beautiful. But part of me wanted to say, "Yeah, but I've had to fill the cracks in with gold from my own resources—financially, physically, spiritually. You all were part of my breaking and not part of my healing." Instead, I felt like they thought it was my fault that I fell apart.

Cindy felt that while overt sexism and sexual harassment tapered off as she entered her forties, she continued to feel dehumanized, stating, "I'm not sure that people actually had more respect for me and they certainly did not feel any obligation to treat me in a humane way or to be held accountable."

Body Taking Me Out

There were instances in which the women's chronic exposure to physiological stress and abuse left their bodies physically debilitated, to the point that they could no longer function and in some cases needed immediate medical attention. Sarah shared that the deterioration of her mental and physical health caused her to reframe her sense of spiritual calling and ultimately decide that "God doesn't call us to be eaten alive":

> It literally took my body taking me out to alert me that this was enough. The toll it took on my mind and my body and my spirit was just so drastic. It's really something that I'm even a functional human being after all of that. And after the deterioration mentally that I went through after the second death threat, I finally saw that God doesn't want this for me. I really got to the point where I realized, this is not a calling. God doesn't call us into things where we are literally eaten alive by toxic people or life-threatening situations. That's not why God calls us into ministry.

Cindy described laying "flat on the floor so that I could stop spasming" as a turning point in no longer wanting to hear from others that she wasn't "working hard enough":

> Shortly after we had reopened after the pandemic, I had a herniated disc and I had surgery. I was still working, but I was working from my couch, because I could not get from my couch to my bathroom without laying down flat on the floor so that I would stop spasming. There was no way for me to come into church. We were still hybrid, everything was happening online and in-person at that point. So, I was doing everything just online and I found out that people were having an issue with that and thought, "Oh, she's not working." I am literally breaking my back for you people. And that was another shift of not willing to put up with people never thinking that I'm working hard enough. It just wasn't worth it to me anymore.

Staying Will Kill You

For some of the women, they were not able to fully recognize the damaging realities of their ministry contexts until they were no longer able to physically function. For others, witnessing colleagues and clergy family members die due to the unsustainable conditions of pastoral leadership, heightened their awareness that one's life was literally "on the line." Several women described the life and death reality of staying versus leaving, including LaVerne who noted:

It's very sad. It's literally disgusting that the church even years after I've left is in the same space. That it drains you. It can kill you. It doesn't care that you're dead. They've done nothing different.

Miranda echoed this feeling with currently active clergy women in mind:

Do not sacrifice yourself on the altar of the church. It will not be there. It will not be there at your deathbed. It's a great perspective builder. Just think, who do you want to be at your deathbed? Well, if you continue to sacrifice yourself there, you will be dead and they won't be there.

Cindy noted having generally good physical health but began developing significant health issues due to chronic stress while in ministry. A few months after leaving active ministry a medical check-up revealed that all her blood tests returned to normal levels, alerting her how much the congregational dynamics had taken its toll on her body:

For the first time in my life, I had much higher blood pressure. I was also having digestive issues. So, my doctor was checking me out for IBS and my back hurt, my feet hurt, my whole body. I was in pain all the time. I thought, do I have some sort of autoimmune disease? I was so fatigued. I just had all of these things and I had really high anxiety and I'm not an anxious person generally speaking. I had never experienced anxiety like this before, but I was just constantly activated in that church. Once I left, the health tests returned to normal.

Deciding to Leave

The level of agency exhibited by each woman depended on their individual circumstances, but overall, the conditions for most of the women were no longer physically and/or emotionally tolerable. Consistent reasons for leaving included concerns for safety, feeling pushed out or scapegoated, and physical and emotional depletion. The social processes connected to the women's decisions to leave a specific pastoral job or active ministry altogether included *vulnerability in betrayal, throwing my hands up,* and *saving my life.*

Vulnerability in Betrayal

The feeling of betrayal was consistently expressed by the women, considering their strong beliefs in what it means to serve alongside others in a shared community of faith. While many of the women felt that they had realistic expectations of the challenges of ministry, they ultimately were shocked and deeply disappointed by the mistreatment, aggressive targeting, and lack of accountability that occurred within their ministry contexts. Haley, who felt relatively prepared for ministry having been raised by parents who were both pastors, described the feeling of institutional betrayal:

> I think overall one word for it is a sense of betrayal. The vulnerability in betrayal. I just feel like I have been wall-up again and again by challenges that felt very gendered and had a lot to do with being undermined and not taken seriously. I was mistreated in ways that I would not tolerate in any other setting. When I realized that was the case, I saw that the work

was costing too much and I could no longer tolerate that. I realized that the church is the last place that I should tolerate this kind of treatment.

Jenny, who also felt her leadership was "being undermined," went to a trusted colleague within her denomination whose response felt like the "nail in the coffin" for Jenny in terms of institutional complicity:

I shared with her how things were unraveling and she said, "You know what? It sounds like some pastoral visits in people's living rooms is what's needed." And that was the nail in the coffin for me on the institution. Here I'm being—I mean abused. That's what I want to say. I don't know if that's accurate, but I feel like I'm being verbally, emotionally, psychologically—I don't know what other kind of word, abused by these people. They are treating me inappropriately. And your response to what I should do is for me to go to their home? And make myself vulnerable in their living room, for what? To receive more verbal abuse from them? What is this?

There was a recognition among the women of how easily church institutions can harm, which often guided the women's more inclusive and trauma-informed approaches to leadership. Christy described this awareness, sharing:

I don't want the church to be an institution who has put someone in a corner and is belittling them and making them feel small. And the church is so good at doing that and I only want to be a part of a church that is expansive and celebrates people for who they are. I think it was a shock to my call as an ordained person. I thought, I'm being taken advantage of because I'm a youth leader and within the structure I have less power. But if I could just get ordained, then I would be in a space within the institution that I could advocate for myself.

But the places where I would have advocated for myself and others weren't working. So, I found myself being hurt by the institution in the very way that I don't want the church to be hurting people in the world.

Rose described the sense of betrayal in her denomination's outward presentation of social justice yet inward "antiquated dehumanizing marginalizing system":

The deeper I got into the system the more I realized that the more things change, the more they stay the same. We were still operating in the same oppressive, antiquated, patriarchal, misogynoir that I saw growing up. It was couched within this beautiful stance of outward social justice, but inward it was still the same antiquated dehumanizing marginalizing system. I suffered in silence. I conformed. And I didn't say anything. For fear of retaliation or fear of being blackballed or fear of being ostracized. So, I watched. And in my silence, I became complicit in the behavior. The way I was able to reconcile what I had learned in seminary, unfortunately, was to leave.

Throwing My Hands Up

As described earlier, the clergy women exhibited varying levels of agency and personal decision-making amid the dehumanizing social dynamics they faced. Self-advocacy efforts were particularly evident when it came to the women's decisions to leave their ministry contexts. In the cases of overt scapegoating and executive derailment, some of the women felt they were unable to leave on their own terms, and were effectively "pushed out" or forced to resign. In these instances, the women felt they ultimately had no choice but to "throw my hands up" and surrender. Kay described multiple issues coming to a head during a staff review meeting in which:

Others were trying to get me to admit I was wrong and the hill I decided to die on was the issue of kids in the sanctuary. I'm never going to ask a parent to remove their child from worship. I'm just not gonna do it.

Kay felt shamed and humiliated as others watched her pack up her office. After "throwing my hands up," she reclaimed her sense of dignity by "stripping the altar":

It felt like I was just yanked, I didn't leave well, and didn't say goodbye to anybody. But I was so sick and I was so worn out and I was so done trying that I just threw my hands up and I said, okay. My parents came to help clear out my office because I couldn't lift stuff because I was still so sick. The church wiped my computer. They felt like they needed somebody on property to watch me as I packed up. It was terrible.

After the last board meeting, I remember thinking, I don't think I'm gonna be here on Sunday and I want my scarves back from the communion table. So, I went up and stripped the altar and sat in the sanctuary by myself eating the loaf of communion bread that I had brought for everybody.

Sandra felt there was simply nothing she could do, once the denominational representative agreed to let the church end her contract:

The board sent me a letter requesting my resignation during Christmas week, which was in violation of the congregation's constitution. They didn't have the authority to do that without a congregational vote. But the denomination told them that they did. I mean, who can I go to, if the denominational rep thinks that they can do these things, and there's no one else for me to go to, to keep them accountable? After very hostile meetings they made very clear that my staying wasn't going to be an option.

Ongoing conflict and verbal attacks became the tipping point for several clergy including Deborah who noted, "It became untenable for me to do that work anymore because of these constant conflicts and attacks. And so, I just resigned."

Saving My Life

The category of *saving my life* reflected utter desperation in which the women's lives were at risk, as well as a powerful expression of agency and no longer tolerating chronic abuse within their ministry contexts. For many of the women there was a realization that there was no defense and no form of protection, particularly with regard to issues of physical safety. Hope resigned from her position because the church was "refusing to take my safety concerns seriously." Similarly, Sarah noted, "It became clear to me that these people didn't have my best interest at heart. No one was going to take care of me in this except me, and that armed police officer out in the lobby." Cora described her realization that no one was going to save her and that she had to make that choice herself:

> I remember at key moments this strong desire to be saved, for someone to notice all this happening and to fix it and to save me. I saw it play out in my faith, I saw it in my vocation, I saw it in my marriage. I even saw it play out in therapy. My therapist is the most incredible person who refused to give me the answer and tell me what to do. But I finally realized nobody was coming to save me. I needed to make the choice to save myself.

The need to save oneself was also felt by LaVerne, who retired from her denomination on her own terms and empowered others to do that same:

> I didn't leave, I retired. I waited until the annual denominational meeting and wrote my formal statement of retirement. I

said that I did not lose members because I didn't push them away. I didn't steal money because I didn't raise any. I made it sound very, very me. The day I retired, a colleague of mine came up to me, literally crying and saying, "LaVerne, how could you leave me here?" I said, "You can go too." She's finally at a position years later where she's more seriously considering stepping away because it is becoming finally too much. More than too much.

Rose also used the language "retire" as opposed to "leave," which enabled her to reclaim her voice and agency while at the same time acknowledge how the "ills of the church were impacting me personally":

At the annual meeting, you heard this big gasp in the room because I didn't tell anyone and I just followed the process for how to state your retirement. And I think everyone was so shocked, they could have objected, but they didn't because they were surprised. And I released a statement, stating that I retired because of the ills of the denomination. It wasn't just bashing and berating the church, there were some great things that came out of it. But I said I was not called to fight those ills that were impacting me personally. So, I had to remove myself and hope that others will find their call to fight the good fight in the denomination. That retirement was a moment of reflection and a moment of regaining my power, my agency, my voice, my call. My body, my mind, my soul, my choice. I reclaimed all of that and left.

GENDERED SCAPEGOATING AND MIMETIC RIVALRY

The negative perceptions others held of the clergy women's presence, personhood, and overall approach to leadership, led to intense blame, bullying, and targeting, which significantly threatened the clergy women's physical and psychological safety and interpersonal boundaries. As noted above, the clergy women's experiences pointed to three stages of escalation, as system anxiety swelled around them. Based on the women verbatim interview language, the three sequential phases included *lightning rod, scapegoating,* and *ousting the threat* (see Figure 5.4).

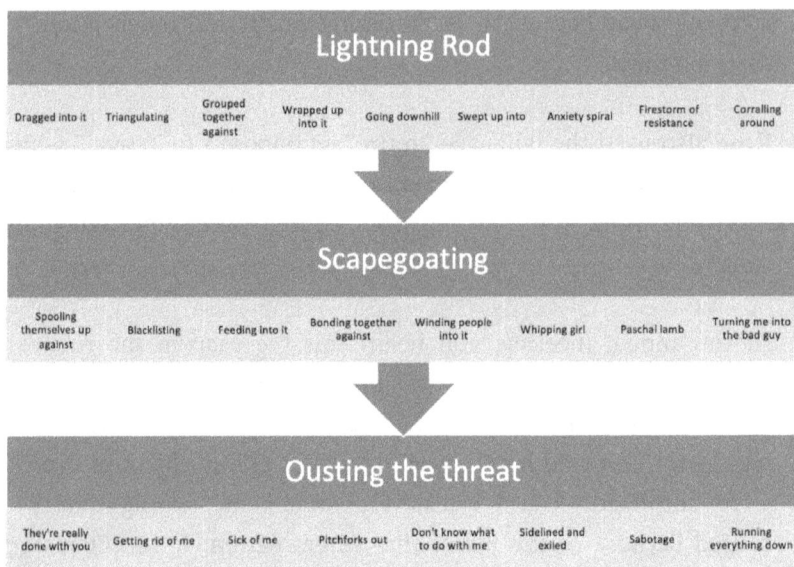

Figure 5.4: Interview Language Representing the Lightning Rod Effect, Scapegoating, and Ousting the Threat

The explanations parishioners used to justify such treatment included accusations of the women's financial misconduct, mental instability, or micro-managing, each of which were inconsistent with the women's self-understanding of their leadership and their otherwise positive reputations within their ministry contexts. Beneath these surface-level accusations were scapegoating behaviors grounded in others' perceptions of the women as a "dissident daughter" and "emasculating disruptor." As outlined earlier, the primary catalysts for the scapegoating mechanism were older women with internalized sexism and insecure men with self-understandings of authoritative masculinity. However, what enabled the scapegoating phenomenon to build momentum and legitimacy without resistance was the inability of the surrounding church and denominational systems to hold the smaller group of disaffected leaders and parishioners responsible for unjustly shifting blame onto the targeted clergy woman.

Alongside this focused group of opponents were several enabling factors that caused the scapegoating mechanism to proceed unchecked, including: 1) loyalty toward a charismatic leader despite acknowledgement of the leader's abuse of power; 2) the familial nature of Protestant church culture and parishioners' desire not to implicate their close friends, or denominational leaders not wanting to undermine their professional colleagues; 3) not wanting to admit or address the church's financial instability and shifting blame to clergy whose salary drew the majority of church funds; 4) political conflict and latent conservatism within the church system regarding social justice and inclusivity; and 5) the perceived otherness of self-differentiated of young clergy woman creating a lightning rod effect that magnified system anxiety (see Figure 5.5).

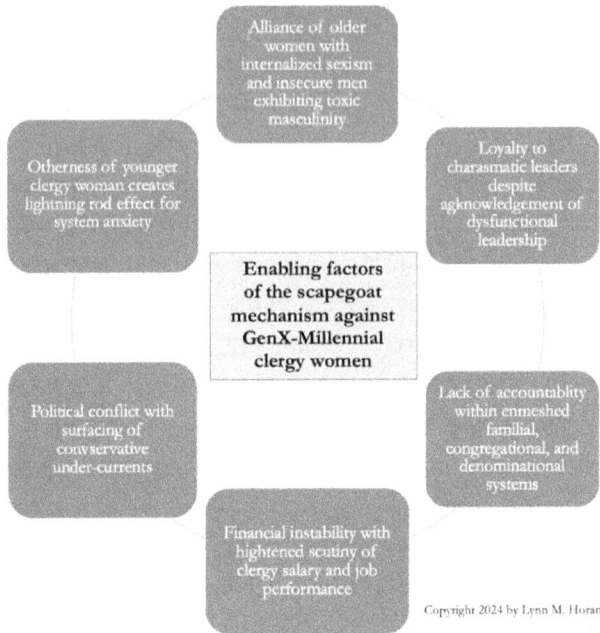

Figure 5.5: Enabling Factors of Scapegoating Mechanism against Gen-X/Millennial Clergy Women

The combined effect of these factors created a perfect storm that centered around a more self-differentiated clergy woman, making it difficult for her to both defend herself personally and professionally or find sufficient pathways of institutional advocacy within her congregation and larger denominational system. The women themselves did not enter these spaces of leadership with a desire to intentionally disrupt or rebel against established community and social norms. To the contrary, their approaches to leadership were deeply relational, collaborative and inclusive, while also promoting mutual accountability and upholding healthy and appropriate boundaries. As a result, the women felt extremely blind-sided and disoriented by the scapegoating mechanism that was activated around them and were often not fully aware of what was happening amid the building tension.

Likewise, those participating in the scapegoating mechanism may not have been fully conscious of what they themselves were engaging in, as their emotional projection was rooted at a deeper level of subconscious rivalry. Finally, those observing the scapegoating mechanism were either ignorant of the underlying dynamics or preferred to avoid conflict rather than defend the targeted clergy woman, therefore contributing to the unchecked momentum of this destructive social process.

Mimetic Theory and the Scapegoating Mechanism

In reflecting on the escalating social conflict surrounding the leadership and identity of self-differentiated Gen-X/Millennial clergy women, the findings of this study strongly align with mimetic theory and the scapegoating mechanism, outlined by French cultural theorist René Girard (1966, 1977, 1986, 1987). A highly nuanced and interdisciplinary theory, the central argument is that human beings are both imitative and rivalrous. Those who we seek to imitate can become our rivals, which can result in intense conflict and violence. A brief mention of Girard's understanding of human rivalry was noted in Roberts' (2016) autoethnography as an Anglican woman priest, where she discussed the unique pressures that female-bodied clergy encounter when ministering within predominantly male-centered leadership contexts. She applied Girard's mimetic theory to explain why leaders within hierarchical institutions are often revered for their ability to provide a sense of safety and belonging, yet are at the same time an object of envy of the desires of the followers. When a social norm is challenged, as is the case with Anglican women priests and increasingly younger women clergy in American Protestantism, Roberts argued that "anxiety arises and the leader is replaced" (p. 81). While Robert's exploration of mimetic rivalry was extremely brief and somewhat oversimplified, it put Girard's theorizing on the map for the more systemic scapegoating of Protestant clergy women addressed in this study.

The term "mimetic" points to the imitative tendency within human social behavior. Girard (1966) argued that what we want or desire does not simply emerge within ourselves as autonomous individuals, but is a social process whereby our desires are inspired by or modeled after the desires of others. Mimesis often operates relatively peacefully among persons in a relationship with clear hierarchy such as parent-child or teacher-apprentice. Such relationships involve a safe psychological distance between persons, which ideally promotes non-competitive, learning interactions. Mimetic desire can also promote social cohesion when the teacher or model is removed either histori-cally or spiritually, for example the relationship between Martin Luther King Jr. and present-day racial justice advocates (Frost, 2021). However, when boundaries and social distinctions are more blurred and the proximity and similarities between the subject and model become more closely related, such as Protestant pastor-parishioner relationships, there is increased potential for what Girard (1966) referred to as mimetic rivalry.

Following an initial period of mimetic rivalry is an escalation of interpersonal conflict that ultimately leads to the scapegoating mecha-nism. Girard (1966) noted, "It is not simply or only that we desire another's possessions, but rather we come to desire the being of another" (p. 83). This intensity of needing to be, become, possess, or control the model reflects much of what the clergy women described as they were surrounded and targeted by a small group of opponents. The women described specific individuals trying to publicly devalue or denigrate them, having been perceived by some as a threat or conta-gion within the larger community.   Building on Girard's mimetic theory, the expulsion of the scapegoat leads to a period of superficial peace through a kind of cleansing or harmonizing ritual. As Fleming (2014) noted, "In a situation of heightened sensitivity to mimetic suggestion and burgeoning conflict, an accusatory gesture is all that is required to unite (and hence to reconcile) warring parties around a common enemy" (p. 4). This was consistent with the clergy women's experiences, as there was no formal discussion or process of account-ability within the congregational or denominational systems leading up to or following their exits.

While the women's experiences reflected a chaotic and disori-enting experience, Redekop (2002) argued that the scapegoating process is not accidental, with the identity of the scapegoat being far from arbitrary. Redekop (2002) offered five specific qualities which scapegoaters either consciously or unconsciously observe in a potential scapegoat and are used to guide and/or justify the scapegoaters' behavior and accusatory narrative. These scapegoat qualities include: 1) perception of difference, otherness, or alterity; 2) perceived difference is felt as a threat to one or more human identity needs within an individual or group of individuals; 3) the scapegoat has some level of power, whether that is in the form of a leadership position or unique identity, which enables the scapegoating process to have an impact on the crisis; 4) the scapegoat must also be considered illegitimate, in terms of their positional or symbolic power, so that the scapegoat action appears justified; and lastly 5) the scapegoat must be vulnerable and unable to counterattack or seek reprisal, revealing the injustice of the scapegoat mechanism (p. 92).

These scapegoat qualities are by no means meant to excuse the scapegoating behavior or justify the blame placed upon the scapegoat. Instead, these qualities point to the distinct social dynamics surrounding the scapegoat's perceived identity and role within the surrounding social system. When applied to the context of Protestant church culture, there is a hyper-mimetic nature to parish ministry due to its high boundary permeability, thick climate of conflicting gender narratives, emotional projection of parishioners, and expectations of feminized servanthood. This creates an extremely precarious environment for self-differentiated women leaders and increased potential for the scapegoating mechanism against Gen-X/Millennial clergy women. As outlined in Table 5.3, Redekop's (2002) scapegoat qualities aligned with the identities of the Gen-X/Millennial clergy women in this study, which further reinforced the potential for systemic scapegoating.

Scapegoat quality	Application to clergy women
Observance of **difference**	Age, gender, firmer boundaries than previous generations of clergy, decentralizing approaches to leadership
Difference perceived as a **threat**	Increased autonomy and boundaries threaten certain individuals who maintain strong gendered expectations of the self-sacrificial woman and its overall function in maintaining church culture
Position of **power** via leadership role and/or unique identity	Clergy role signifies educational, spiritual, theological, and positional power, privilege, and prestige
Considered **illegitimate**	Positional power and decision-making capacity conflicts with gendered narratives of women's relationality, compliance, and passivity
Vulnerable with no available recourse	Ineffective or nonexistent congregational accountability structures, complacent denominational leadership, and church-state separation prevent judiciary buffer against scapegoating mechanism

Table 5.3: Application of Redekop's (2002) Scapegoat Qualities to Gen-X/Millennial Clergy Women

A compelling argument of Girard's mimetic theory is that the catalyst for the scapegoat mechanism is not a menacing difference but a threatening sameness. Girard (1986) argued that "persecutors are never obsessed by difference, but rather by its unutterable contrary, the lack of difference" (p. 22). This study revealed that mimetic rivalry and the subsequent scapegoating mechanism is based on a complex tension between sameness and difference. This tension surfaced in various ways, depending on the identity of scapegoaters. For specific older women who rejected the clergy women in this study, what appeared to be most threatening was the physical sameness of another female-bodied individual, yet one with a greater sense of autonomy and agency. For specific men, the threatening sameness may have centered around the clergy women's self-actualized leadership capabilities, qualities that the men felt should have been reserved exclusively for them but which they lacked in their own personal lives.

This study revealed that the most vocal opponents of the clergy women expressed a dangerously fragile sense of self, which reflects Reineke's (2009) analysis of scapegoating as a "conflict associated with a lack of being" (p. 249). The clergy women's primary opponents may have felt stifled or erased by the presence, personhood, and agency of a younger self-differentiated woman leader. The reflection of someone who was similar to them, yet who exhibited a more fullness of being, magnified their own deficiencies and deeply felt insecurities. The younger clergy women represented someone that they longed to be or become, and the proximity of that possibility yet impossible attainment necessitated the rejection and subsequent removal of the clergy women in order to preserve one's own limited sense of being. This understanding of a loss of being due to a threatening sameness helps to explain the drastic shift that took place for clergy women who were well-respected and, in many cases, beloved by the larger congregation and surrounding community, but who eventually became vilified and derailed by a small disaffected group of parishioners and denominational leaders.

Gendered Scapegoating

Girard theorized that the scapegoating mechanism was a phenomenon that functioned irrespective of gender divides, arguing that all individuals are capable of scapegoating as well as being vulnerable to being the scapegoat (Eggen, 2013, p.189). An important advancement in mimetic theory has been the work of Girardian feminist scholars such as Reineke (1990, 1992, 1997, 2014), Adams (1993), Novak (1994), Weir (1996), and Rike (1996), who have explored the ways in which social constructions of gender influence the scapegoating process. Recent applications of Girard's original theory also include Reineke's (2014) exploration of familial trauma, Moore's (2021) research on White supremacy and racial violence, and Frost's (2019) exploration of attachment theory and relational conflict.

While Novak (1994) argued that androcentric interpretations of mimetic theory have the potential to re-victimize women by silencing their experiences, Rike (1996) problematized assumptions that women can only be victims and not perpetrators of scapegoating. Rike pointed out that while women have been scapegoated throughout history, "Not all women end up as victims of violence and the rituals constructed to appease it, nor do women remain simply victims of the tides of violence: many repeat the cycle of victimization and them-selves become perpetrators" (p. 22). This is particularly true when applied to the mother-daughter wound in Protestant church culture, in which internalized sexism of certain older women leads to negative perceptions of the younger clergy woman as a "dissident daughter" in need of reprimanding. However, as Hasseldine (2017) pointed out, such resentment on the part of certain older women is not necessarily grounded in malicious intent but is more likely influenced by their own lived experiences of being restricted and silenced by systemic gender oppression in their own lives.

While the application of mimetic theory is not restricted to reli-gious contexts, there is a strong precedent for the use of mimetic theory to examine socio-religious dynamics, particularly when it comes to patriarchal social systems with strong sacrificial theologies. A powerful example of this is Reineke's (1990) analysis of the gendered scapegoating that drove the Salem witch trials in seven-teenth-century New England, in which women who were widowed or did not have male heirs were disproportionately targeted as their more independent social status threatened traditional land inheritance prac-tices and amplified surrounding religious and economic anxieties. Reineke's observations provide a chilling connection to the systemic scapegoating of Gen-X/Millennial clergy women in contemporary Protestant church culture, where younger clergy women's increased agency and autonomy threaten persistent cultural narratives of female servitude. While this is a striking comparison, it is important to acknowledge that while gendered scapegoating of self-differentiated women leaders is heightened within socio-religious communities with rigid gender norms, such scapegoating behavior is also prevalent in non-religious professional settings and familial relationships.

Feminist applications of mimetic theory have a vital capacity to unveil the silencing, secrecy, and shame associated with the scapegoat mechanism within highly patriarchal social settings. Exposing the social processes involved in scapegoat expulsion makes it such that the human community can no longer claim naivete from or abdicate responsibility for the violence that underlies socio-religious ritualization (Novak, 1994, p.22). Instead, as Rike (1996) asserted, feminist scholarship holds a mirror before us all as to the ways in which we perpetuate, even if passively or unconsciously, the scapegoating mechanism. Feminist Girardians reveal that the omission of gender has the potential to silence and, therefore, revictimize any identity who experiences systemic othering.

The human proclivity toward mimetic scapegoating is played out in direct and indirect ways in both conservative and progressive religious communities, as well as in non-religious culture and leadership contexts. In conservative religious contexts, anxiety about women's autonomy is directly expressed through overt sexism and sexual harassment of women clergy as well as formal denominational rejection of women's ordination (Rocca, 2023). However, in mainline American Protestantism where gender equality is generally promoted and women's ordination is well-established, anxiety regarding women's agency and autonomy is expressed through more insidious forms of systemic scapegoating, executive derailment, professional defamation, and institutional gaslighting. The scapegoating mechanism within Protestant church culture is often left undetected due denominational complacency and ineffective accountability structures, as well as the separation of church and state, which prevents these harmful and dysfunctional behaviors from being publicly addressed.

Based on these persistent yet often silenced social dynamics, it is important to shed light on the process of systemic scapegoating of Gen-X/Millennial clergy women, in order to more effectively advocate for those who are currently experiencing this level of dehumanization and abuse. While gendered scapegoating is pervasive within Protestant church culture due to high boundary permeability and conflicting gender narratives, these social dynamics are also evident among self-differentiated women leaders in non-religious contexts with persistent patriarchal narratives.

6

RECONSTITUTING SELF

Upon leaving dehumanizing and abusive ministry contexts fraught with feminized servanthood and gendered scapegoating, each of the clergy women began the painstaking process of healing and recovery. After addressing their immediate needs related to physical health and post-traumatic stress, the women embarked on the deep work of metabolizing their feelings of institutional betrayal and taking gradual steps to establish new understandings of self, spirituality, and community. Returning to the explanatory matrix outlined in Chapter 4 (see Table 4.1), these experiences were reflected within the final category of *reconstituting self.* Each of the participants acknowledged a multi-layered process of self-discovery and self-acceptance that continues to evolve as they process the impact of their ministry experiences on their personal, psychological, physical, relational, and spiritual lives.

METABOLIZING, EMBODYING, REMEMBERING

Within the category of *reconstituting self* were specific areas of deep self-reflection including *metabolizing feelings, embodying uncertainty,* and *remembering who I am* (see Table 6.1). Discussed below in detail, this

185

important interior work involved earlier life experiences, pivotal moments in ministry, deconstruction of religious understandings, and profound existential questions of identity and self-worth.

Primary Dimension	Conceptual Categories and Corresponding Social Processes		
	Metabolizing Feelings	**Embodying Uncertainty**	**Remembering Who I Am**
Reconstituting Self	• Finding truth in emotions • Recovering from trauma • Letting go of guilt and shame	• Questioning self and identity • Is the church good? • Healing takes time	• Unlearning conditioned responses • Tending to what I want • Saving and liberating self

Table 6.1: Primary Dimension: Reconstituting Self

Metabolizing Feelings

Finding Truth in Emotions

The women expressed how crucial it was to acknowledge feelings of anger, sadness, and grief, as they were often expected to absorb others' emotions and minimize or silence their own emotional responses in their pastoral leadership roles. Through the help of a therapist, Allegra began recognizing and embodying her emotions more fully and honestly:

> I've been having to do a lot of grief work. I was really angry for a long time and I couldn't place why I was feeling so angry. But I find myself finally having to deal with my emotions because I kept just sort of blocking them out, like there's this little box that I had them in. My therapist really helped me to understand that it's okay to feel things and to embody that.

Deborah also expressed the need to process feelings of anger and grief, while also accepting the possibility of "alternative endings":

> It's been hugely liberating to not have to craft a self-aware and caring response to parishioners who are actively harming me. I'm just angry about it. The difference now is that, as my therapist has shown me, there's an alternate way for it to end. When

it was in the moment and it was happening, I was just stuck there. No one was my advocate. I had no promise of safety or way through that included anyone else having my back. But now, that's not true anymore. I don't have any obligation to stay there. I have no investment in the system that does this to women in particular. There's a lot of grief around that too, but I have more freedom to get angry and notice I'm angry and also understand I don't have to be angry anymore.

Recovering from Trauma

Most of the women noted some form of professional therapy as an important part of their recovery, with some women engaging in specific trauma therapy, including tapping, EMDR (eye movement desensitization and reprocessing), and trauma-informed spiritual direction. Joanna experienced how the technique of tapping helped "rewire her brain" when she felt triggered while driving past the church:

I had been able to avoid driving by the church since I left, but one night there was just no way to not drive by the church. And I had a lot of catastrophic thoughts about driving by the building. I'm in my car thinking, "You're anxious about this but you love yourself and you accept yourself." I went through all my tapping and I made it past the church and I've done it a couple times since then and it's gotten better. Those muscles and that stress response to that congregation have gotten better.

Marta, who used EMDR therapy while still in active ministry, found it both helpful in processing the trauma of working with a psychologically abusive senior pastor, but also alerted her to the fact that her work conditions had become intolerable:

I told my therapist and he said, "I've been doing therapy over 30 years. This is one of the worst examples of leadership I have ever heard in my office." He's said, "This is terrible." And we did EMDR trauma therapy over it because it was so affecting me. That was helpful, but I also thought, I shouldn't work in a place where I have to go to trauma therapy because of my boss.

Letting Go of Guilt and Shame

Several women described feelings of guilt and shame, which they intentionally worked to reframe, particularly as others around them validated their experiences. Kay described feeling like a failure, particularly after hearing from a denominational leader, "I was really excited for your ministry there. I put you there because I thought you would do so well." Kay was able to let go of some of her guilt by surrounding herself with people who know her true self, and who "can see me and remind me who I am." Cora, who felt more isolated in her recovery, was grateful for a team of health care providers who acknowledged her experiences:

At that time, my relationship with my own personal faith was just destroyed. I mean, I was so low. Nobody had even acknowledged that I had left. I didn't feel like a human, I just felt like this shell of everything I had. That I had failed. That I had not been able to make it. But nobody cared about it. I'm so thankful that both of my health care providers gave me good resources to be able to support me during that time.

Sarah felt that the "nightmare" experience of two death threats during her ministry was her fault, but over time came to understand that she was not to blame:

For a long time, I really wrestled with, is this my fault? What could I have done differently to not become a target, to prevent this from happening? Did I jump too far in trying to save this woman? And to this day, I wouldn't have done anything different with her. My walking alongside her, my advocating for her, my showing up for her, I wouldn't have done anything different. I don't feel like I crossed a boundary, which then led to this nightmare. The nightmare was her husband and not because of my actions. I couldn't have controlled what he did.

Embodying Uncertainty

Questioning Self and Identity

A common experience among the women was a profound existential re-evaluation, one that continues to evolve, in which the women are questioning their sense of worth, their purpose in life, their spiritual orientation and beliefs, their leadership abilities, and their overall identity. Cora spoke of her "entire life being enmeshed in the church," but has found greater peace in the idea of "embodying uncertainty":

> I vacillate between the designation of atheist and agnostic because I just don't think it's that important to know what I believe on any given day. And it's really liberating to not have that be a part of my job. To be able to explore that in my own way, in my own time without having to package it for someone else. Or to not carry the burden of certainty anymore. The idea of certainty was a huge transition point for me. Being okay with not knowing. Being okay with not being certain.
>
> I think in ministry there was a fear that if I did not embody certainty, that if I did not embody faith fully that there's something wrong. I'm trusting myself to live in this uncertainty for the rest of my life and I think there's something really terrifying about that. There used to be this comfort of certainty and being told that I have a place in this huge thing. And now, that thing is really nebulous, whatever I'm a part of, whatever we're all part of. I'm practicing being more tolerant of the unknowing.

LaVerne asked herself difficult questions about whether her time in ministry was a waste but has come to understand her path as always oriented around teaching and equipping others:

> I wonder if I've wasted my life, wasted my education, wasted my time. My mom will often ask me, "Why'd you get all those degrees if you aren't using them?" But if I had done the military for twenty years, you wouldn't be asking me this. Why is this different? Because it's God related? So that kind of gets people off my back sometimes. But I always had the teaching element. I like to equip people with tools that they can utilize to function practically, whether that be spiritually or literally.

Haley described reclaiming her sense of self as no longer needing to "perform femininity" in ways that denied her nonbinary identity:

> Trying to fit less into the box of femininity has been really healing for me. I feel like some of the masking I was doing, performing this role as a young clergy woman, was tied into performing femininity. And it was really soon after leaving ministry that I realized that I didn't have to under the circumstances. I didn't have to perform that and I no longer wanted to and I was no longer willing to.

Allegra described the process of reconstituting self as deeply connected to her identity as a woman:

> I'm starting to embody who I actually am instead of who I thought I had to be to fill a role. I'm embracing my inner goddess. I'm like a beautiful glass of wine that's finally reaching its bloom, like how grapes take time before they can reach that. I feel more grounded in who I am and not apologizing for that. This is who I am.

Is the Church Good?

Leaving toxic church culture caused many of the women to question the purpose of the church and to re-evaluate their own religious beliefs and practices. Some no longer identify as Christian and have become more agnostic or non-theist, while others maintain core beliefs in a higher power while choosing not to participant in church life or organized religion. Others have taken on an exploratory stance in which they remain spiritually open but in new ways.

Joan questions whether the church is "good" and continues to discern whether it's something she will want to engage in as the looks to the future:

My whole spiritual understanding was framed on the importance of the church and living life together, whether I'm pastoring or not. I had a deep love for the church. And so, I started to wonder, is the church good? Then I started to wonder is my faith good? If my faith is founded on following God in community and this is what community looks like when it's trying to follow God, then something must be wrong somewhere in that equation.

Allegra feels that she has been freed from a religious system that she no longer believes in:

The church is a human construct. And while I strongly believe in the divine, I'm realizing that my understanding of that is very different than it used to be. I feel like I've been freed up to not have to live into should or could or would. Or an orthodoxy that I don't believe in anymore. But instead, to be able to experience the divine in a more freeing and open way. And also learning that there's possibility in that. But it's scary because it means that you're stepping away from tradition and expectations. But maybe it's time to do that and maybe that's what's happening with other people around me and that's freeing, that openness.

Healing Takes Time

The women described their healing and recovery as an ongoing process, which they continue to navigate. Joan shared, "I feel like after this number of church abuse cycles, I'm not in crisis about it. I'm just waiting. Eventually, I always I end up with what's next. And I just haven't gotten there yet." Sandra, who worked part-time with an outdoor sporting company after leaving the ministry, found it to be a "graceful place for me to just do the healing that I needed to do":

> They were very patient with me. They allowed me to be my broken self and when I was doing a little bit better, I was invited to lead and do some of that visioning stuff that I know I'm good at. It was a very graceful place for me to just do the healing that I needed. Even though a number of the folks there are non-religious people, nobody ever said, "Well, that's what you get for being part of church. You know, this is why the church is so horrible." They respected that it was important to me and they might not understand it but they knew that I needed to figure out how to heal from it without their judgment.

Remembering Who I Am

Unlearning Conditioned Responses

Several women discussed the process of letting go or unlearning conditioned ways of being and relating to others that they had absorbed within their ministry contexts, as well as through their families of origins and overall societal expectations. Allegra described learning to distinguish between her authentic voice and "voices I had internalized for myself":

I definitely had an internal monologue where I asked myself, "Why are you feeling that way?" Or "What's going on? You need to knock that off." They weren't my voices, but voices that I had internalized for myself. I felt like my soul was being chipped away, and I wasn't able to function. I wasn't acting out of a deep authentic place. I was playing a character, or a role of a person. But it wasn't me. Now I'm in a place where I can fully experience my emotions and not judge or shame myself for feeling them.

Vivienne described the ongoing process of rewriting the narrative of "not being enough":

I think when you are gaslit continuously, when you are beaten down over and over and told that you're not enough, it becomes part of a narrative that's really hard to break free from. I'm working really hard to re-write that.

Cora began to question the sustainability of a belief system based on "triumphing over trauma":

I think my whole life I have found meaning in triumphing over trauma, whether it was excelling in school or extracurricular activities. That has been part of my story that I have reflected on. And I think in the church, as an extension of my own faith development, if I just do this right, if I just do this well, God is gonna take care of me. It's a narrative that I deeply question now because it causes such harm.

Tending to What I Want

The process of leaving dehumanizing and abusive ministry contexts placed many of the women in a completely new and unfamiliar space of being able to make their own decisions on their own terms, based on their own unique wants, desires, and preferences.

Several women observed how they had to painstakingly re-learn how to make independent decisions that were not restricted by the highly rigid expectations and pressurized nature of congregational culture.

Jenny described daily practices that helped her identify what she wanted after constantly tending to others' needs while in ministry:

> I had no sense of my own personal way of existing in the world anymore. It was all conformed. After I left, at first, I felt I needed to have no obligations and just do the first thing that came to my mind and just do that. If I wanted to reorganize my closet, spend the day and do that, and if I wanted to clean underneath my bathroom sink, just do that.

Sarah's work as a hospital chaplain has been extremely healing for her because of the spaciousness it offers for spiritual curiosity:

> I think it helps get me through that trauma. And also, as a chaplain, it's working in a place where I serve people of all and no faiths. I get to enter into their space without hearing "Nope, this is how we do it here." So, I feel like a spiritual explorer in a lot of ways. My faith is about wandering and I'm curious and what if, and you don't have to follow the party line.

Deborah has found it liberating to use her voice more honestly, and to embrace freedom of thought and expression in her writing:

> In my post ministry writing I get really excited when I use profanity or say things that I would never preach in a pulpit. It's not just freedom of expression but freedom of thought. I allow myself to think down roads that I wouldn't have in ministry because it wouldn't be productive or it wouldn't feed a sermon or a Bible study or a pastoral conversation. But I don't have any of those restrictions now and I'm not obligated to stay within anybody else's lines anymore.

Since retiring from her denomination, a message that LaVerne has told herself and others is to:

Remember yourself on purpose. That was the one thing that I had lost in a couple of different ways in my life, but just remembering who I am and why I am. That was the most important thing and being okay with that, even if that did not present in the manner that everyone thought it should.

Saving and Liberating Self

Beneath the day-do-day experiences of making one's own decisions and reclaiming one's identity apart from the harmful dynamics of congregational ministry, many of the women found within them a powerful capacity to save themselves. With new understandings of both theological and social liberation, the women came to see themselves as their sole and primary advocate in ways that they had not be able to access or promote as a clergy. Cora described her journey of self-actualization as learning "to save myself," based on a growing sense of her own value and self-worth:

I realized nobody's coming to save you, Cora. You have to save yourself. Nobody's coming to fix this. Nobody is going to take you away from this and heal everything. You get to decide to do that. It's ridiculous how much self-limiting talk, especially as women, we're conditioned to have with ourselves from the time that we're tiny. It wasn't until I was in my thirties, that I began to have a conversation with myself about my worth and about my value. That it was okay to love myself.

Haley began to find a sense of "wholeness and integrity" within her own body, which she hadn't experienced while in ministry:

During therapy I had this really deep experience of self. I returned to myself, myself in my intersex body that I had been pushed out of. In my young personhood I had been subjected to these normalizing medical procedures. And I was brought back to myself and my feeling of wholeness and bodily integrity and how I am in the world. And I was no longer willing to deny the okayness of who and how I naturally am.

Rose described the process of "seeking liberation within myself" as a driving force in her path beyond ministry:

I finally said enough. This is not a womanist tenant. I need to seek liberation within myself. I need to honor myself and love myself and acknowledge my gifts. I have the agency to decide how I use my gifts. I was able to reconcile the Spirit in me with what I felt externally called to do. And I realized the church was not it, not in this way.

RECLAIMING PERSONAL AND LEADERSHIP STRENGTHS

As each of the women shared their continuing process of recovery and reclaiming of self, a common thread was acknowledgment of their own personal and leadership strengths. Drawn from early life circumstances, varied professional backgrounds, and educational and seminary training, the women shared their personal commitments and leadership priorities, both in and beyond active ministry. Several core leadership strengths were identified, including decentralizing power, inclusivity and bringing voices to the table, power-with instead of power-over, transparency and mutual accountability, and relationality alongside healthy boundaries (see Figure 6.1).

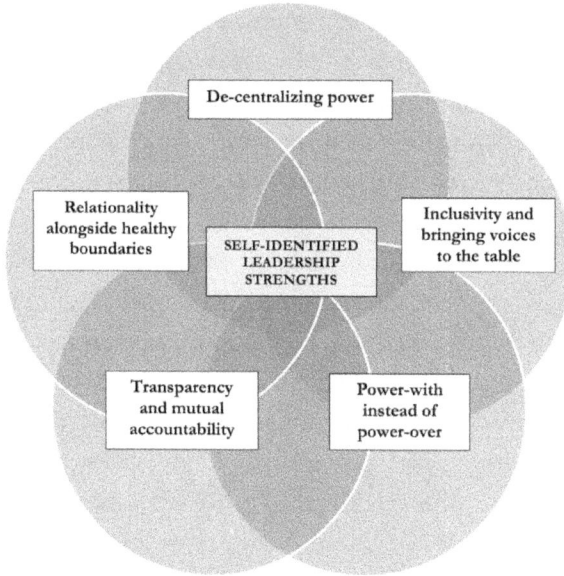

De-centralizing power

Relationality alongside healthy boundaries

SELF-IDENTIFIED LEADERSHIP STRENGTHS

Inclusivity and bringing voices to the table

Transparency and mutual accountability

Power-with instead of power-over

Figure 6.1: Self-Identified Leadership Strengths of Gen-X/Millennial Clergy Women

The clergy women viewed their intentional leadership approaches as positive community-building skill sets that were generally well-received within their ministry contexts and also crucial for their own survival within their surrounding toxic environments. However, the women also felt that their efforts to work collaboratively, de-centralize leadership, and promote mutual accountability were met with significant resistance and opposition. It became evident that those who sought to delegitimize the women's leadership abilities were those who had benefited from patriarchal models of power, ego, and control of a single narrative. As addressed in Chapter 5, the traits that made the clergy women effective leaders and skilled communicators grounded in a deep sense of self, were the very same qualities that were perceived as threatening and destabilizing for certain individuals with a human identity need for female subservience. While the women saw their leadership approaches as important expressions of self-actualization both for themselves and others, these approaches were highly criticized by those with a fragile sense of self who preferred more linear, power-over, and hierarchical leadership models.

For clergy women who experienced gendered scapegoating, an important part of their recovery process was re-claiming the strengths of the scapegoat identity. It is important not to interpret the scapegoating mechanism merely as a way to reveal or hone certain leadership skills or character traits, which will be discussed further below in terms of problematizing resilience. Instead, this discussion honors the highly evolved qualities evident in scapegoats, while at the same time interrogating the scapegoat mechanism itself. Figure 6.2 outlines the specific strengths observed in the clergy women who experienced gendered scapegoating: 1) honesty, integrity, and truth-telling; 2) independent thinking and unwillingness to automatically follow; 3) courage and willingness to speak out on issues of injustice; 4) emotional strength and resilience; and 5) self-differentiated and not easily manipulated. While these qualities were exhibited in varying degrees by each of the women clergy, they were more pronounced for those women represented in Narrative A (see Table 1.1 above). Such personal and leadership strengths proved to be threatening to eventual scapegoaters, which reinforced the need to re-claim these qualities after the women left their abusive ministry contexts.

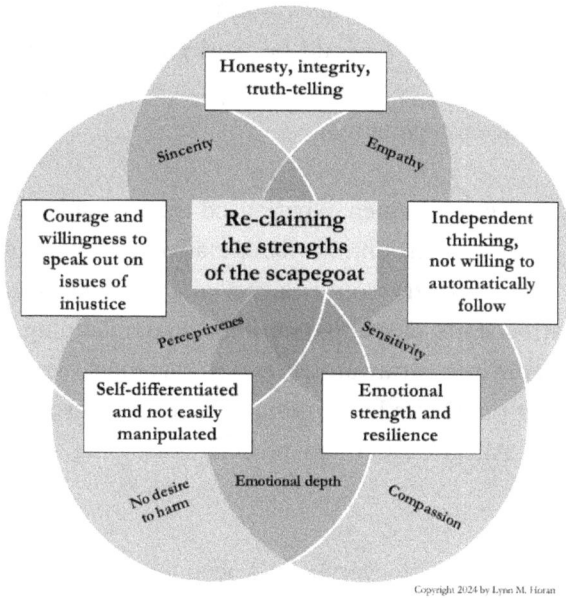

Figure 6.2: Reclaiming Leadership Strengths of the Scapegoat

As pastoral leaders, both those in more senior level positions and those in associate pastor roles, the women generally exhibited such traits as sincerity, empathy, perceptiveness, sensitivity, emotional depth, compassion, and lack of motivation to hurt or harm. These qualities are often inherent to the role of pastor and within other care-giving, service-oriented professions. However, the women in this study experienced heightened levels of criticism, cruelty, and judgement on the part of other clergy and congregants, which ultimately took advantage of these more humanistic traits. Jenny recalled a conversation she had with a friend near the end of her ministry that enabled her to see these dynamics more clearly:

I was talking to a friend about my frustrations with the church and she said, "Jenny, they're taking advantage of you. This is why you're so upset." I had a hard time even taking that in because I just assumed that we're all in this together to serve. It never occurred to me that people would want to control the narrative in that way. I had always heard of that but I just didn't think that the people I would be working with would be that way. It was the first time that it really occurred to me that they were taking advantage of me.

Many of the clergy women experienced the two-sided coin of identifying and at times confronting manipulative and abusive personalities within their ministry contexts, yet at the same time exhibiting highly empathic traits of compassion and understanding. Ultimately, the women became hyper-aware of the interpersonal dynamics in their midst, and over time were less willing to excuse or absorb the destructive behaviors. Allegra described no longer needing to fix a broken system, noting:

I'm not in charge of everybody's feelings. Not everybody is gonna like me. It is not my responsibility to save the church. We all were handed a shitty card anyways because this stuff was already breaking apart. And it's not my role to fix what other people have already broken.

Similarly, Cindy felt that:

My attitude started to shift at that point. I was no longer willing to deal with people's crap and people projecting all over me. I'm done with that. I have a life of my own. And that feeling only grew as I encountered some of these things.

In addition to the core leadership strengths shared by the women, and the resulting push-back that many received, the women exhibited highly nuanced levels of embodied knowing. This was expressed through emotional intelligence and awareness of one's own felt experiences in relation to others. The women described intense somatic experiences when confronted with others' emotional projection yet were also able to make deliberate choices to promote their own psychological and physical safety. Allegra described embodied awareness as something that evolved gradually for her, after addressing her own conditioning to not "take up space":

It just never occurred to me that I was allowed to have space. I'd been so conditioned to be a helper and to be a shadow, to back down. It just never had occurred to me that, of course, I'm allowed space. That's a basic human right. You're here on this earth. You need space to be you. So, take it.

Embodied knowing also emerged when the women described chronic psychological abuse in their ministry settings. Elsa shared detailed imagery of what this felt like in her body:

It was like a pit in my stomach, almost like the bottom was falling out. Like on an elevator whose cable gets cut or if you're on a roller coaster, right after you get to the top and you start the descent. There's this sense of "oh my god," and my hands would get clammy. And it got to where I don't even remember when that would happen. I got so conditioned to it that it didn't surprise me. I felt almost bulletproof because it was just like, you suit up and that's part of the job, I guess. Fighter pilots shit their pants regularly when they reach a certain mach speed. And I felt like at some point it's like, yeah, I'm covered in shit, whatever, that's part of the job.

The women's attentiveness to their own embodied experiences, enhanced the women's leadership capacity and also alerted the women to a "felt sense" (Cornell & McGavin, 2021, p. 29) of when their psychological and physical safety was compromised. In exploring the topic of embodiment, I do not intend to essentialize women as being inherently feeling-oriented or more aware of their embodied experiences than other individuals. However, I do recognize that this was an important element of the clergy women's experiences, which informed their leadership approaches and decisions. These elements of embodied knowing represented a meta-level of engagement that reinforced the women's other leadership strengths, and also supported the women in their process of reclaiming and revaluing their core identities after leaving toxic ministry settings.

BEYOND RECKONING AND RESILIENCE

The research participants expressed that the process of *reconstituting self* was and continues to be a complex and multi-layered experience, including elements of institutional reckoning and individual resilience. The terms "reckoning" and "resilience" are often used within the context of social justice and trauma recovery, but can be problematic and incomplete as it relates to agency and victimization. My intent throughout this research was to acknowledge the women's reality of victimization and expose the dehumanizing treatment they endured, while at the same time honoring the women's desire to move beyond victim mentality in ways that do not inappropriately glorify experiences of resilience.

The term "reckoning" has entered public discourse in important ways over the past few years, particularly in relation to increased awareness and social activism regarding sexual abuse and harassment (Hirshman, 2019) and racial justice (Norris, 2020). A reckoning literally means a "settling of accounts," often in terms of a business or legal transaction. However, when it comes to the lived experiences of individuals who have endured social injustice and dehumanizing abuse, the idea of reckoning is not as cut and dry. As Norris (2020) pointed out with regard to racial injustice, "A reckoning by definition refers to the moment when we finally deal with an ugly situation. It is more than just admitting that there's a problem." Norris (2020) urged those involved in the work of social justice to use the word "reckoning" with caution as it can inaccurately, and in some cases dismissively, assume that the work has been accomplished. Hirshman (2019) used the term reckoning as an "epic battle" as she outlined the history of litigation against perpetrators of sexual abuse and harassment, while at the same time acknowledging the need for continued advocacy work and public awareness.

With these understandings in mind, the experiences of the women in this study depicted neither a final "settling of accounts," which assumes that the realities have been sufficiently addressed, nor an "epic battle," as the women are currently prioritizing their own personal paths of recovery as opposed to addressing the issues of institutional betrayal in a formal organized way. As Cindy noted, there was a need to move forward in her life rather than reforming an institution that she no longer wanted to engage with:

I realized these are things that should not be happening to me and that have happened in various incarnations over and over in multiple churches that I worked in. And I'm just no longer interested in dealing with it. What changed was me, not the church.

Haley described no longer feeling compelled to change a system that "costs too much":

In my recovery I have been trying to let myself off the hook for not changing the system from within, knowing that it just costs too much. The system did not have enough to support me in doing that difficult work of changing the system from within. If I had just been compensated fairly, that may have made a difference. That would have gone a long way in my ability to stay and fight some of those fights. But without that floor and without enough allies on these fronts, it just costs too much.

The research findings and analysis from this study do serve as a form of collective reckoning, as this is the first rigorous qualitative study that examines feminized servanthood and systemic scapegoating of Gen-X/Millennial clergy women in American Protestantism. While this is a productive step toward institutional and cultural change, it is also up to each of the individual women who experience these dynamics to determine her level of involvement in exposing these realities, and the extent to which it feels safe and/or meaningful within her own process of recovery. Such a decision is highly individual and deeply personal and should not be imposed on survivors of this kind of trauma and abuse.

Whether or not the women in this study and others who have encountered similar dynamics choose to engage in any formal kind of institutional reckoning, it is important to take account of the costs, primarily those experienced by the clergy women themselves, but also the costs to the congregations they left. The costs identified within the compiled clergy interviews include: 1) emotional and psychological trauma; 2) religious trauma and institutional betrayal; 3) challenges seeking alternative employment; 4) financial hardship for clergy women and their families; 5) lack of legal recourse; and 6) congregational chaos and confusion (see Figure 6.3).

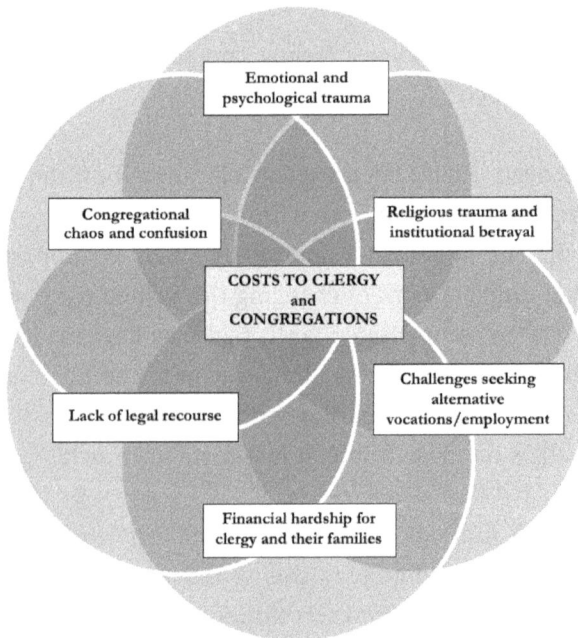

Copyright 2024 by Lynn M. Horan

Figure 6.3: The Costs of Feminized Servanthood and Gendered Scapegoating

Emotional and Psychological Trauma: Dehumanizing and abusive experiences of feminized servanthood and gendered scapegoating continue to be detrimental to the emotional well-being of younger women clergy, who are extremely competent, compassionate, and ethical leaders, and generally well-respected in their parish contexts and surrounding local communities. The extreme rejection of their pastoral identity on the part of a handful of individuals led many of the women in this study to experience debilitating anxiety and depression while still in their ministry contexts, with continued emotional trauma in the immediate aftermath. Ongoing psychological damage includes questions of self-worth, doubt in one's spiritual calling, and deep questioning of one's overall faith journey. Institutional gaslighting, silencing, and shaming of younger women clergy, at both congregational and denominational levels, also led to the women's inability to trust larger denominational systems. These social and institutional dynamics have left the majority of the clergy research participants no longer interested in continuing a pastoral vocation and ultimately leaving active ministry.

Religious Trauma and Institutional Betrayal: For those who were able to recover emotionally, financially, and professionally from clergy scapegoating, the impact of religious trauma involves a much more difficult path of recovery. The majority of the research participants noted the inability to walk into a church without feeling emotionally triggered. As a result, most of the research participants avoid attending worship service or affiliating with any faith-based community, which can be especially challenging for those with clergy spouses and/or children who have developed a personal connection to church life. For those clergy with children, there is a constant negotiation of how to present the realities of toxic church culture in a way that still honors their children's spiritual curiosity and understandings of faith.

Challenges Seeking Alternative Vocations or Employment: For the women who ultimately decided to leave ordained ministry, financial necessity coupled with a desire to recuperate their professional identity caused them to seek alternative employment. Many of the women have perused vocations in non-religious fields such as teaching, counseling, social work, and human services, while others have made a more direct departure from caregiving professions and have embarked on new careers including environmental advocacy, real estate, and entrepreneurial ventures. However, having been in congregational ministry for several years, in addition to typically three years of seminary education, most of the women have found it difficult to pivot professionally, regardless of one's alternative career choices. Despite the diverse skillset, managerial acumen, and highly developed emotional intelligence required of pastoral leaders, former clergy are often viewed with a great deal of uncertainty and skepticism among non-religious employers, requiring former clergy to re-define themselves professionally, often requiring additional degrees or certifications.

Financial Hardship for Clergy and Their Families: While some were more financially able to leave pastoral positions on their own terms, each of the women faced financial challenges. Some felt forced to "voluntarily" resign with imposed non-disclosure agreements, having been told it would protect their future employability as a clergy. Such forced resignations made it difficult for the women to quickly transition into alternative work or ministerial settings in order to make-up for lost income. Due to the inability for clergy to secure adequate investigations of misconduct, executive derailment, and scapegoating dynamics, the clergy women were often denied appropriate severance, which Protestant denominations regularly offer in instances of irreconcilable differences or extreme hardship. In addition, women clergy serving in senior or solo pastor positions were often the primary breadwinners for their families, due to the strong benefit packages offered by mainline Protestant denominations. Clergy who resided in a manse or parsonage immediately lost their housing, which further intensified their financial vulnerability. These financial considerations delayed many of the clergy women from leaving highly volatile congregational settings in the first place, causing them to endure prolonged psychological abuse and institutional gaslighting as they assessed their precarious circumstances.

Lack of Legal Recourse: Due to the separation of church and state, ecclesial leaders, including Protestant clergy, are not afforded protection by anti-discrimination laws in the United States' Title VII of the Civil Rights Act of 1964. This "ministerial exemption" is based on the ecclesial status of ordained clergy, who are generally considered outside of the bounds of secular legal protection (The Pew Forum, 2011). This leaves women clergy with little to no legal recourse against such abuses as sexual misconduct, harassment, unsafe work environments, and breaches of contract, thereby placing clergy women in a vulnerable and, in some cases, dangerous leadership space. Such areas of conflict are left to be addressed by internal judicatory processes led by denominational leaders, who are often ill-equipped or actively reject the claims brought forth by clergy women (Greene & Robbins, 2015, p. 406). While separation of church and state is deeply valued within contemporary society, the inability of clergy to pursue legal counsel or recourse when faced with unsafe work conditions, gender discrimination, sexual harassment, and professional defamation, is an extreme professional hazard to working as an ordained clergy.

Congregational Chaos and Confusion: While the focus of this research was the experience of women clergy themselves, the dehumanizing and abusive treatment of clergy women also has a negative impact on the entire congregational system. In the wake of hostile scapegoating, forced, or expedited resignations, and the resulting expulsion of a pastoral leader, there is a lack of open communication and closure, which leads to dysphoria and silencing within the congregational social system with many innocently asking, "Why did she leave?" As outlined in Girard's (1986) mimetic theory, the scapegoating process operates as a seemingly cathartic, cleansing act that removes perceived dangerous elements and results in a false sense of calm, unity, and cultural homogeneity. This temporary peace is a deceptive veil that further silences the realities of dehumanizing treatment, inhibits genuine dialogue, and prevents behavioral and cultural change. Without the ability to critically reflect on these dynamics, congregations are often unable and at times unwilling to address unhealthy relational patterns that will inevitably affect future pastoral leaders, particularly other clergy women.

Problematizing "Resiliency"

Just as discussions of "reckoning" can be oversimplified in ways that deny the root causes of injustice, one-dimensional understandings of "resilience" can also promote further harm. I do not intend for this research to reinforce the age-old notion of "iron sharpening iron," which inappropriately interprets the clergy women's traumatic experiences as an exercise in developing thicker skin for the challenges of ordained ministry. The idealized image of the "bounce-backable woman" is especially detrimental, as it minimizes experiences of trauma and abuse as a character-building struggle along a broader path of self-discovery (Gill & Orgad, 2018). Similarly, it is problematic to focus on the notion of "grit" as it disregards the systemic issues that result in the need for such perseverance, and "inappropriately clears the power structure from responsibility toward increasing equity" (Roberts, 2022, p. 197).

In light of these limiting perspectives, I approached this research through a feminist critical lens that understands resilience as a multi-layered and non-linear experience that 1) acknowledges actual harm; 2) interrogates existing structures of oppression; and 3) prioritizes individual agency and subjectivity. This more expansive approach to resilience was echoed by the clergy women participants as they continue to process the abuse and institutional betrayal they experienced, while at the same time intentionally reclaiming their core values and identities.

Within this more complex view of resilience is the understanding that trauma recovery is an embodied process. Just as experiences of trauma manifest themselves in our physical bodies, the process of recovery also occurs at a deeply somatic level (Van der Kolk, 2014). As Menakem (2017) states, "Contrary to what many people believe, trauma is not primarily an emotional response. Trauma always happens in the body. . . a wordless story our body tells itself about what is safe and what is a threat" (pp. 7, 9). As discussed earlier, the importance of embodied practices of trauma recovery were reflected in several of the women's use of various pyscho-somatic therapies such as EMDR (eye movement desensitization and reprocessing) and tapping, which helped the women metabolize their experiences of psychological abuse. Others engaged in embodied catharses such as long-distance running, yoga and other forms of movement, in order to "re-set" their bodies following their exits from ministry. Such move-ment-based practices are increasingly used within the field of trauma recovery, based on Stephen Porges' (2011) polyvagal theory and the important use of embodied practices to reshape nervous system responses to past trauma (Dana, 2018).

This study promoted a trauma-informed understanding of resilience that centers the survivor as an "embodied psychosocial subject" who navigates the recovery process with agency and decision-making power (Aranda et al., 2012, p. 548). The clergy women's varied experiences of recovery challenge one-dimensional understand-ings of resilience that focus on a fixed endpoint when one suddenly feels healed or whole. Rather than view resilience as being "found" or "made," which diminishes individual agency and subjectivity, the women in this study experienced resilience as an ongoing and evolving process of self-actualization. The women understood their own process of recovery not as a final word of hope and redemption but as a painstakingly carved out path of survival and self-awareness.

In each of the interviews, the women questioned simplistic under-standings of resilience and instead described the complex nature of their own recovery process. Jenny described the difficult work of "rein-venting herself" after leaving a toxic ministry context:

> After feeling guilty about using the word "abuse," I feel liber-ated to use it. If what I experienced was abuse then it's easier to see that how I felt and my struggles to cope were not my fault. It wasn't a lack of resilience or strength. It was the reality of working in a toxic environment.
>
> You never get used to breathing poison—you have to

remove yourself from it in order to feel better. It changes my feelings from cowering in shame, to standing tall and feeling proud of what I was able to accomplish in the midst of that abuse and toxicity. It also makes me feel angry because I would have loved to have my whole career in the church, and now I have to reinvent myself. There's liberation in that, but also sadness and anger that it's even necessary.

Many of the women expressed wanting to no longer perpetuate victim mentality, yet at the same time needing to acknowledge the intense mistreatment to which they were subjected. Cora powerfully described this interplay between concrete elements of victimization and reclaiming a sense of agency and choice:

When I was thinking about this interview, I was very clear that I didn't want to be seen as a victim. What I've focused on is that in every moment of this process, I was the one that made the choice to step away. I was the one that made the choice to stop. I can't do this. Nobody made me do anything. All along, it was me saying, I know there's a better choice than this. And so, with that choice, I also see the insecurity of, "I did this to myself, for a period of time." Over the years I've had to learn to trust myself in a way that I had never trusted myself before. And once that process began, I could own my decision without blaming myself for the aftermath.

Throughout this study, I sought to center the women's voices and promote emancipatory research that addresses oppressive social systems and relational dynamics. At the same time, I wanted to highlight the women's leadership strengths, decision-making capacity, and deep self-awareness that developed throughout their experiences in and beyond ordained ministry. Each of the women were deeply affected by the experiences that they went through, as they continue to do the hard work of trauma recovery and reconstituting of self. Many voiced that what they went through was unjust, a response that

I echo as both a feminist researcher and former clergy. Therefore, I am cautious of any discussions that attempt to minimize or deflect the women's lived experiences of trauma, in order to present a cohesive story of healing. In sharing this research, I have intentionally avoided overly hopeful or redemptive conclusions, and instead prefer to let the women's voices and experiences speak for themselves.

Theoretical Model

This research journey began with the question: *What are the lived experiences of Gen-X/Millennial clergy women who have left active ministry because they felt that their interpersonal and professional boundaries were violated or their physical and/or psychological safety was threatened?* Despite working in denominations with an established history of women's ordination, the clergy women in this study experienced overwhelming barriers to the full acceptance of their pastoral leadership. Alongside the painful realities that the women faced, they also exhibited powerful self-actualization that took place both within and beyond their ministry contexts. Each of the dimensions and categories outlined above reveal varying levels of agency and self-actualization that the women were able to enact despite the intense interpersonal and institutional challenges of their individual ministry contexts.

The harrowing experiences that the women shared were harmful and debilitating in heart-wrenching ways, yet there was a very evident process of reconstituting self that included self-driven healing and empowerment beyond church culture and ordained pastoral leadership. The research findings outlined above inform the final theoretical model illustrated below (see Figure 6.4), which is discussed in further detail in Chapter 1.

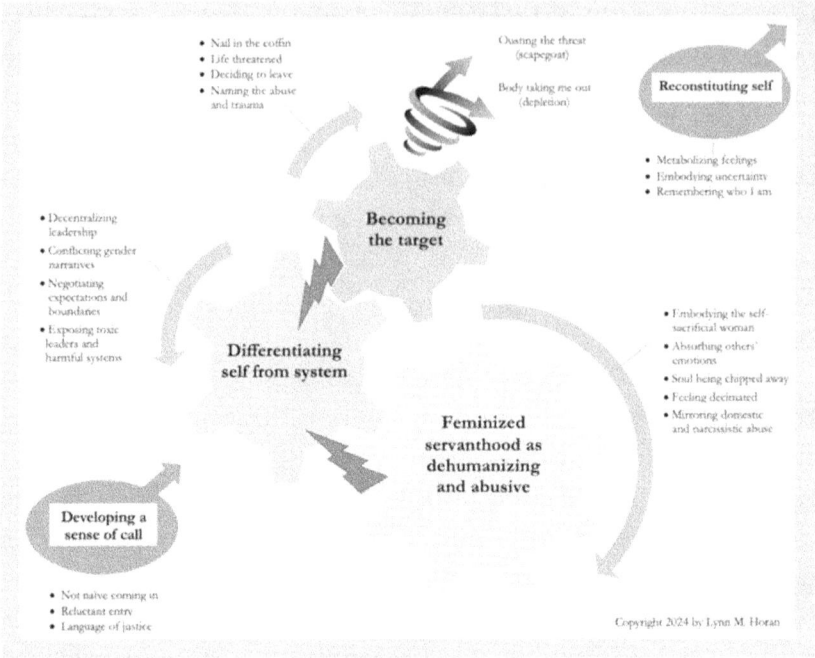

Figure 6.4: Theoretical Model of Feminized Servanthood, Gendered Scapegoating, and the Disappearance of Gen-X/Millennial Clergy Women

Both leadership scholarship and public discourse have taken on the question of executive turnover, emotional burnout, compassion fatigue, and work-life balance as it relates to women leaders in a variety of professions. However, only recently, have discussions on gender bias in the workplace (Diehl & Dzubinski, 2016), managerial derailment of women leaders (Bono et al., 2017), and push-to-leave forces (Dwivedi et al., 2023) exposed the double bind expectations that women leaders face. This study built on these observations by addressing why younger self-differentiated clergy women who exhibit healthy and appropriate interpersonal boundaries are being systematically scapegoated and dehumanized within mainline American Protestantism. This body of work presents new social theory drawn from the research findings, in order to explain "What *all* is going on here?" (Schatzman, 1991). The final theoretical propositions drawn from this study include: 1) feminized servanthood and the shadow side of servant-leadership; 2) negative perceptions of younger clergy women as a "dissident daughter" and "emasculating disruptor"; 3) gendered scapegoating and the disappearance of self-differentiated Gen-X/Millennial clergy women; and 4) reconstructing self beyond reckoning and resilience.

Based on certain limitations within this study, there is a need for further research on the intersectional identities of clergy women particularly Women of Color and non-binary clergy, which were under-represented in this study. In addition, further longitudinal research is needed to explore the ongoing recovery process for women leaders who have experienced institutional betrayal, executive derailment and/or systemic scapegoating within their professional contexts. Continued qualitative research in these areas have the potential to promote more egalitarian and human-centered institutions where younger women leaders can work and thrive.

AFTERWORD

Hesitant Hope

I knew at the onset of this research that I would encounter experiences that reflected some of my own journey in and beyond ordained ministry. However, I felt stunned and deeply saddened by the extent to which the abusive conditions severely compromised the women's physical and emotional well-being. There was genuine pain, unjust treatment, unnecessary harm, and undeniable abuse. Having worked with survivors of domestic violence, I have heard women say that the only hope is that they "got out." I believe this applies here. The remaining questions of hope are for each individual clergy woman to determine for herself, along her own path of recovery.

In centering the clergy women's perspectives, many of the research participants shared that participating in this study helped them to more fully embrace their decisions to leave, and to further release feelings of grief, anger, and shame. Others felt that the interview itself allowed them to find their voice again, in a powerful and life-giving way. On a communal level, thanks to the courageous women in this study, there has been a growing community of survivors and advocates that has coalesced around this work. It is clear that the experiences shared by the clergy women in this study reflect systemic issues across American Protestantism. This research provides validation, solidarity, and guidance for those who are facing similar forms of relational and institutional conflict.

In terms of institutional change, time will tell. As this research is shared among local congregations, denominational leaders, and seminary institutions, my hope is that it will encourage others to question existing narratives that negatively impact younger clergy women, and create opportunities for concrete institutional and behavioral change within Protestant church culture.

Denominational Reform

Based on the findings of this study, there are several specific areas of institutional change that would create more safe and equitable spaces for ordained clergy women: 1) professionalize and adequately train church and denominational human resource entities to fully recognize the dynamics of feminized servanthood and gendered scapegoating; 2) expand seminary curriculum to address forms of intergenerational and gender-based conflict that are pervasive within Protestant church culture; 3) promote efforts toward clergy unionization in light of church-state separation and the lack of legal recourse for clergy who experience workplace harassment and discrimination; 4) increase denominational advocacy in cases where weak regional church governance re-victimizes clergy women who are seeking support; 5) standardize severance negotiation practices including the elimination of non-disclosure agreements; 6) require ongoing boundary training for congregations that is comparable to that which is required of ordained clergy; and 7) build congregational awareness and the need for cultural change with regard to ingrained gender-identity narratives and their harmful impact on the psychological safety and interpersonal boundaries of younger clergy women.

APPENDIX: TEN TOOLS FOR LEAVING TOXIC CHURCHES

1. Your Experience is Real

As women we are continually conditioned not to listen to our bodies, to silence our intuitive awareness of our surroundings and relationships, and to deny or minimize our lived experiences. We also live and work in a patriarchal culture that consistently gaslights our perspectives and observations, telling us that our experiences of abuse and dehumanization are not real. If you have felt targeted, bullied, or scapegoated, the trauma of those experiences lives in our bodies. It is real. You have a right to live and work in spaces that don't contribute to that trauma.

2. Protecting Yourself as You Exit

The process of leaving a toxic ministry context is similar to leaving an abusive relationship. For survivors of abuse, the most dangerous time is typically once the decision has been made to leave, up until the actual exit. When a clergy woman makes public her plans to leave, she may experience heightened targeting, scrutiny, blame, and scapegoating. Depending on the circumstances, it may be safest to minimize one's contact with the congregation and avoid being in the church building as much as possible. It is also wise to refrain from explaining your exit and offering pastoral care to those who are exhibiting unhealthy emotional projection. If possible, it is helpful to secure a trusted advocate(s) during contract and severance negotiations, and, if available, to acquire legal and/or police protection (despite these services often being denied to clergy due to church-state separation).

3. A Community of Survivors

During and immediately following one's exit, finding a community of support is an essential piece of the recovery process. Due to the systemic nature of these dynamics, there is a growing community of clergy women survivors, including those who participated in this research. Each survivor has valuable knowledge and experience regarding the healing process, finding alternative employment, addressing pastoral identity and sense of call, and re-building one's life following church-based trauma. To learn more about available support groups and individual coaching visit:

Young Clergy Women International: https://www.facebook.com/youngclergywomen/

Clergy Women Crisis Recovery: https://www.lynnhoran.com/clergy-women-crisis-recovery.html

4. Healing Takes Time

The process of healing and recovery takes time, and some days (or weeks, or years) may be more difficult than others. Healing is not a linear process, as trauma lives in our bodies. Women who have been dehumanized in their leadership contexts may find that such mistreatment brings to the surface previous hurts and instances of abuse. Taking seriously the healing process means committing time and energy to our recovery process. It is a worthwhile investment that will enable us to begin healing at the root of our pain and to make important choices in our personal and professional lives moving forward.

5. Therapy Works

Having a trusted therapist is an essential part of recovering from church-based trauma. Throughout the recovery process, there may be continued triggers that stand as obstacles to regaining a sense of wholeness. It is also important to identify additional therapy modalities to support you through the different layers and seasons of your recovery. Embodied therapies may include yoga, physical exercise, and other somatic work that help release traumatic memories stored in specific muscle groups. Cognitive therapies may include journaling, reflective writing, and guided reading. Other healing pathways may include artistic outlets or leadership and life coaching that center on re-writing harmful narratives and reclaiming one's core values. A multi-faceted and holistic approach to trauma recovery can address the many aspects of self that are affected by trauma and psychological abuse and ultimately build pathways for more sustainable healing.

6. Remember Your Passions

What did you love before the world told you what to be or how to act? It's a hard question to ask ourselves because it causes us to admit that we may have lost aspects of our true self somewhere along the way. Entering a meaningful vocation, such as pastoral ministry, is steeped in the language of calling and purpose. But there are other aspects of self that reside outside that call that may have been neglected or pushed aside. What have you missed doing? Who have you missed being? Take small steps to re-capture those passions and identities.

7. Small Circle of Trust

A heavy societal expectation is placed on women to be relational at all costs, absorbing others' emotions to the detriment of our own well-being. In leaving a toxic ministry context, you have an opportunity to change that narrative by selecting who you avail yourself to, at what level of engagement, in what context, and for how long. An important part of recovering from oppressive church culture is to build strong boundaries with those who may not understand or may question your decision to leave. This will enable you to cultivate an inner circle of trust, in which you identify specific individuals with whom you feel safe and seen. This space of acceptance and validation allows you to intentionally develop a clear sense of what you will and will not tolerate in relationship with others.

8. Reclaim Your Leadership Strengths

Experiencing church-based abuse can cause many clergy women to ask "What did I do wrong?" or "What could I have done differently to prevent this?" While self-reflection is an important part of the recovery process, self-blame can be extremely harmful. Alternative lines of questioning may be "What did I do well in this call?" "What are my leadership strengths?" Overall, the leadership strengths exhibited by younger clergy women are often what are seen as most threatening to others within toxic congregational systems. Finding communities and alternative employment where those strengths are valued is an important part of the recovery process.

9. Own Your Story

During your exit and in the immediate aftermath, there will be those who will try to deny, minimize, gaslight, or silence your experiences. Finding those who believe you is critical as you will be able to share your experience in a safe and supportive space. As you move further into your healing and recovery process, you may feel comfortable sharing only certain aspects of your story with certain people. Owning your story means that you get to choose what you share and with whom. Making these deliberate choices can help you regain your own voice and agency as you reclaim your core sense of self beyond toxic ministry culture.

10. You Get to Choose

Just as each of us owns our own story, it's helpful to remind ourselves that these experiences do not define us. It is important to acknowledge that we have been victimized, which holds a much-needed mirror up to abusive and complacent institutions. However, we get to choose how that victimization defines our lives moving forward. You may find aspects of your experience help you make critical choices around future employment and relationships in your life. You may also find that holding onto aspects of your experience are no longer serving you. It's up to you how you choose to incorporate your experiences into your path moving forward and what you chose to let go of. You get to decide.

ABOUT THE AUTHOR

Lynn Horan, PhD, MA, MDiv, is a gender and leadership scholar and professional life coach specializing in women's leadership and life development. She is a contributing author in *Leadership at the Spiritual Edge* (Routledge) and the *Transformational Women Leaders Book Series* (International Leadership Association), where her work focuses on embodied leadership and the psychological safety of Gen-X and Millennial women leaders. As a former Presbyterian clergy and health policy analyst for the New York State Senate, Lynn holds a deep understanding of complex religious and political systems and their impact on social narratives. Lynn is committed to cross-cultural and inter-generational relationship-building, having worked in health education, homeless advocacy, and domestic violence prevention in communities in Southern Mexico, Central Peru, and upstate New York. A trained contemporary dancer and yoga practitioner, Lynn believes strongly in the restorative capacity of movement and embodied awareness as a means of cultivating healing, wholeness and reconciliation in individuals and communities. She currently lives in upstate New York with her husband the three children.

Lynn Horan, PhD Leadership and Life Development
www.lynnhoran.com

Clergy Women Crisis Recovery
www.lynnhoran.com/clergy-women-crisis-recovery

ACKNOWLEDGMENTS

This research would not have been possible without the courageous clergy women, gifted pastors, and transformational leaders who participated in this study and an earlier pilot study as part of my doctoral work through Antioch University's Graduate School of Leadership and Change. Thank you for trusting me with your experiences of religious trauma and psychological abuse that informed your decisions to leave toxic ministry settings, as well as sharing your humanizing leadership approaches, deep emotional intelligence, and unapologetic decision-making, which has blazed a path for others who are facing similar realities. Your words hold power and proclaim the need for concrete change.

Surrounding this group of women is a growing community of clergy women who are transitioning out of abusive ministry contexts. Thank you for supporting and amplifying this work as you pursue your own paths of healing and recovery. For all the clergy women who have journeyed with me, thank you for validating this work through your own lived experiences and for your willingness to share the outcomes of this research with those who are looking for a way out.

To my Antioch colleagues, faculty, and friends, thank you for being such a beloved community and family throughout this important research. Special thanks to my PhD dissertation committee members Dr. Harriet Schwartz, Dr. Martha Reineke, and Dr. Lemuel Watson, who validated this research through their own commitments to trauma-informed leadership and scholarship. I'm also grateful for my trusted mentors Dr. Rachel Roberts, Dr. Susan Cloninger, Dr. Sarah-Jane Page, and Dr. Keli Rugenstein, whose important research on gender and leadership was a guiding light. It has been such an honor to work with each of you and this research is a reflection of the encouragement and expertise you have graciously shared with me.

I am incredibly grateful to Rev. Dr. Angela Yarber and the brilliant editorial team at Tehom Center Publishing, who have supported this work from its early stages and whose ethos of inclusivity powerfully elevates marginalized voices committed to social change.

To my dearest friends, thank you for honoring this work and all that it means. And, most importantly, to my husband, Vince, and my children Margot, Chantal, and Vincent, you have given this work more meaning than you will ever know.

BIBLIOGRAPHY

Adams, R (1993). Violence, difference, sacrifice: A conversation with René Girard. *Religion & Literature, 25*(2), 9–3. https://www.jstor.org/stable/40059554

Ammons, S. (2013). Work-family boundary strategies: Stability and alignment between preferred and enacted boundaries. *Journal of Vocational Behavior, 82*(1), 49–58. https://doi.org/10.1016/j.jvb.2012.11.002

Aranda, K., Zeeman. L., Scholes, J., & Morales, AS-M. (2012). The resilient subject: Exploring subjectivity, identity and the body in narratives of resilience. *Health. 16*(5):548–563. https://doi.org/10.1177/1363459312438564

Baker-Bell, A. (2020). *Linguistic justice: Black language, literacy, identity, and petagogy.* Routledge. https://doi.org/10.4324/9781315147383

Barna Group. (2019, September 14). *Number of female senior pastors in protestant churches doubles in past decade.* Retrieved from https://www.barna.com/research/number-of-female-senior-pastors-in-protestant-churches-doubles-in-past-decade/

Becker, D. (2020). Where has all the context gone?: Feminism within therapeutic culture. In D. Neihring, O.J. Madsen, E. Cabanas, C. Mills, & D. Kerrigan (Eds.), *The Routledge international handbook of global therapeutic cultures* (pp. 400–408). Routledge. https://doi.org/10.4324/9780429024764-37

Becker, P. (2000). Boundaries and silences in a post-feminist sociology. *Sociology of Religion, 61*(4), 399–408. https://doi.org/10.2307/3712523

Bendroth, M. (2022). *Good and mad: Mainline Protestant churchwomen, 1920-1980.* Oxford Academic. https://doi.org/10.1093/oso/9780197654064.001.0001

Bono, J. E., Braddy, P. W., Liu, Y., Gilbert, E.K., Fleenor, J., Quast, L. N., & Center, B. A. (2017). Dropped on the way to the top: Gender and managerial derailment. *Personnel Psychology, 70*(4), 729–768. https://doi.org/10.1111/peps.12184

Bourdieu, P. (1991). *Language and symbolic power.* Harvard University Press.

Burke, E. (2022). *You, me, and us: Exploring early career female psychologists' experience of trauma work* (Publication No. 28648133) [Doctoral dissertation, Fordham University]. ProQuest Dissertations Publishing.

Burnett, R. G. (2017). *The evolution of women pastors in mainline protestant denominations.* [Doctoral dissertation, Western Kentucky University]. http://digitalcommons.wku.edu/diss/119

Burton, J. (1987). *Resolving deep-rooted conflicts.* Lanham: University Press of America.

Campbell-Reed, E. R. (2019). No joke! Resisting the "culture of disbelief" that keeps clergy women pushing uphill. *CrossCurrents, 69*(1), 29–38. https://doi.org/10.1353/cro.2019.a782678

Cataldi, S. (1993). *Emotion, depth and flesh: A study on sensitive space: Reflections on Merleau-Ponty's philosophy of embodiment.* University of New York Press.

Charmaz, K. (2003). Qualitative interviewing and grounded theory analysis. In J. A.

Holstein &J. F. Gubrium (Eds.), *Handbook of interview research: Context and method* (pp. 675–694). Sage.

Columbia Law School, (2017, June 8). Kimberlé Crenshaw on intersectionality, More than two decades later. Retrieved from https://www.law.columbia.edu/news/archive/kimberle-crenshaw-intersectionality-more-two-decades-later

Cornell, A. W., & McGavin, B. (2021). The concept of "felt sense" in embodied knowing and action. In J. F. Tantia (Ed.), *The art and science of embodied research design: Concepts, methods and cases* (pp. 29–39). Routledge. https://doi.org/10.4324/9780429429941-3

Crenshaw, K. (1989). Demarginalizing the intersection of race and sex: A Black feminist critique of antidiscrimination doctrine, feminist theory and antiracist politics. *University of Chicago Legal Forum, 1*(8). Retrieved from http://chicagounbound.uchicago.edu/uclf/vol1989/iss1/8

Dana, D. (2018). *The polyvagal theory in therapy: Engaging the rhythm of regulation*. W W Norton & Co.

Daves, S. (2021). Merleau-Ponty, trans philosophy, and the ambiguous body. *Human Studies, 44*(4), 529–557. https://doi.org/10.1007/s10746-021-09590-7

Diehl, A. B., & Dzubinski, L.M. (2016). Making the invisible visible: A cross-sector analysis of gender-based leadership barriers. *Human Resource Development Quarterly, 27*, 181–206. https://doi.org/10.1002/hrdq.21248

Donnelly, G. (2020). Leading change: The theory and practice of integrative polarity work. *World Futures, 76*(8), 497–518. https://doi.org/10.1080/02604027.2020.1801310

Dowding, K., Lewis, C., & Packer, A. (2012). *The pattern of forced exits from the ministry. In K. Dowding & C. Lewis (Eds.), Ministerial careers and accountability in the Australian commonwealth government (pp. 115–134).* Australian National University Press. https://doi.org/10.22459/mcaacg.09.2012.06

Duffy, B. (2021). *The generation myth: Why when you're born matters less than you think.* Basic Books.

Dwivedi, P., Gee, I. H., Withers, M. C., & Boivie, S. (2023). No reason to leave: The effects of CEO diversity-valuing behavior on psychological safety and turnover for female executives. *Journal of Applied Psychology, 108*(7), 1262–1276. https://doi.org/10.1037/apl0001071

Eagly, A. H., & Karau, S. J. (2002). Role congruity theory of prejudice toward female leaders. *Psychological Review, 109*(3), 573–98. https://doi.org/10.1037//0033-295x.109.3.573

Eagly, A. H. (2005). Achieving relational authenticity in leadership: Does gender matter? *The Leadership Quarterly, 16*(3), 459–74. https://doi.org/10.1016/j.leaqua.2005.03.007

Edmondson, A. C., & Lei, Z. (2014). Psychological safety: The history, renaissance, and future of an interpersonal construct. *Annual Review of Organizational Psychology and Organizational Behavior, 1*(1), 23–43. https://doi.org/10.1146/annurev-orgpsych-031413-091305

Eggen, W. (2013). Girard's gender neutrality and faithful feminism. *Studia Gdańskie. 32,*

189–206. Retrieved from http://cejsh.icm.edu.pl/cejsh/element/bwmeta1.element.desklight- 020d8b36-f34a-4b71-bf1f-828b2d57f44f

Eicher-Catt, D. (2005). The myth of servant-leadership: a feminist perspective. *Women and Language, 28*(1), 17–25. Retrieved from https://www.academia.edu/14264417/The_Myth_of_Servant_Leadership

Ellemers, N., Rink, F., Derks, B., & Ryan, M. (2012). Women in high places: When and why promoting women into top positions can harm them individually or as a group (and how to prevent this). *Research in Organization Behavior, 32,* 163–187. https://doi.org/10.1016/j.riob.2012.10.003

Faraj, S., & Yan, A. (2009). Boundary work in knowledge teams. *Journal of Applied Psychology, 94*(3), 604–617. https://doi.org/10.1037/a0014367

Fleming, C. (2014). Mimesis, violence, and the sacred: An Overview of the thought of René Girard. In J. Hodge, S. Cowdell, & C. Fleming (Eds.), *Violence, desire, and the sacred, volume 2: René Girard and sacrifice in life, love and literature* (pp. 1–13). New York: Bloomsbury.

Florer-Bixler, M. (2021, November 30). Why pastors are joining the great resignation. *Sojourners.* Retrieved from https://sojo.net/articles/why-pastors-are-joining-great-resignation

Frame, M. W., & Shehan, C. (2004). Care for the caregiver: Clues for the pastoral care of clergywomen. *Pastoral Psychology,* 52(5), 369–380. https://doi.org/10.1023/b:pasp.0000020685.13115.57

Frost, K. (2019). Exploring Girard's concerns about human proximity: Attachment and mimetic theory in conversation. *Contagion: Journal of Violence, Mimesis, and Culture, 26*(1), 47–63. https://doi.org/10.14321/contagion.26.2019.0047

Frost, K. (2021). Mimetic theory: A new paradigm for understanding the psychology of conflict. *Christian Scholar's Review, 50*(2), 165–187. Retrieved from https://christian-scholars.com/mimetic-theory-a-new-paradigm-for-understanding-the-psychology-of-conflict/

Gardner, W.L., Cogliser, C. C., Davis, K. M. & Dickens, M. P. (2011). Authentic leadership: A review of the literature and research agenda. *The Leadership Quarterly, 22*(6), 1120–45. https://doi.org/10.1016/j.leaqua.2011.09.007

Gill, R., & Orgad, S. (2018). The amazing bounce-backable woman: Resilience and the psychological turn in neoliberalism. *Sociological Research Online, 23*(2), 477–495. https://doi.org/10.1177/1360780418769673

Girard, R. (1966). *Deceit, desire and the novel.* Johns Hopkins University Press. https://doi.org/10.56021/9780801802201

Girard, R. (1977). *Violence and the sacred* Baltimore: Johns Hopkins University Press. https://doi.org/10.56021/9780801819636

Girard, R. (1986). *The scapegoat* (; Y. Freccero, Trans.). Johns Hopkins University Press. https://doi.org/10.1353/book.98235

Girard, R. (1987). *Things hidden since the foundation of the world.* Stanford University Press.

Glavin, P., Schieman, S., & Reid, S. (2011). Boundary-spanning work demands and their consequences for guilt and psychological distress. *Journal of Health and Social Behavior, 52*(1), 43–57. https://doi.org/10.1177/0022146510395023

Gray, J. S., & Tucker, J. C. (2022). *Presbyterian polity for church leaders, updated fourth edition.* Geneva Press.

Greene, A., & Robbins, M. (2015). The cost of a calling? Clergywomen and work in the church of England. *Gender, Work and Organization, 22*(4), 405–420. https://doi.org/10.1111/gwao.12101

Greenleaf, R. (2002). *Servant leadership: A journey into the nature of legitimate power and greatness 25th anniversary edition.* Paulist Press.

Gross, E. (2022, July 26). The great resignation: Are pastors resigning, redefining or reevaluating? *Faith and Leadership.* Retrieve from https://faithandleadership.com/the-great-resignation-are-pastors-resigning-redefining-or-reevaluating

Gunderson, G., & Chocrane, J. (2015). *Religion and the health of the public: Shifting the paradigm.* London: Palgrave Macmillan.

Gupta, V. K., Han, S., Mortal, S. C., Silveri, S. D., & Turban, D. B. (2018). Do women CEOs face greater threat of shareholder activism compared to male CEOs? A role congruity perspective. *Journal of Applied Psychology, 103*(2), 228–236. https://doi.org/10.1037/apl0000269

Hanisch, C. (1970). *The personal is political. In S. Firestone, and A. Koedt (Eds.), Notes from the second year: Women's liberation. New York: Radical Feminism. Retrieved from* https://www.carolhanisch.org/CHwritings/PIP.html

Hasseldine, R. (2017). *The mother-daughter puzzle: A new generational understanding of the mother-daughter relationship.* Women's Bookshelf Publishing.

Hirshman, L. (2019). *Reckoning: The epic battle against sexual abuse and harassment.* Houghton Mifflin Harcourt.

Holloway, E. L., & Schwartz, H. L. (2018). Drawing from the margins: Grounded theory research design and EDI studies. In L. A. E. Booysen, R. Bendi, & J. K. Pringle (Eds.), *Handbook of research methods in diversity management, equality and inclusion at work* (pp. 497–528). Elgar. https://doi.org/10.4337/9781783476084.00032

Hope and challenge: Vocation within the PC(USA) (May, 2018). *The Presbyterian Outlook.* Retrieved from https://pres-outlook.org/2018/05/hope-and-challenge-vocation-within-the-pcusa/

Horan, L. (2024). Feminized Servanthood, Gendered Scapegoating, and the Disappearance of Gen-X/Millennial Protestant Clergy Women. https://aura.antioch.edu/etds/1063

Hunter, R. (2016, May 24). Presbyterian Church (USA) celebrates 60 years of women clergy: Remembering six decades of pioneering pastors. *Presbyterian Church (U.S.A.)* Retrieved from https://www.pcusa.org/news/2016/5/24/pcusa-celebrates-60-years-womens-ordination/

Jagger, S. (2021). Mutual flourishing? Women priests and symbolic violence in the church of England. *Religion and gender, 11*(2), 192–217. https://doi.org/10.1163/18785417-bja10006

Jalovec, K., Swick, S., Becker, C., & Reifsnyder, R. (2011). When the lightning rod leaves home: a family therapy case characterized by successive generations of familial conflict during a transition into young adulthood. *Harvard Review of Psychiatry, 19*(6), 302–12. https://doi.org/10.3109/10673229.2011.632600

Jonsen, K., Maznevski, M.L., & Schneider, S.C. (2010). Gender differences in leadership – believing is seeing: Implications for managing diversity. *Equality, Diversity and Inclusion: An International Journal, 29*, 549–572. https://doi.org/10.1108/02610151011067504

Jordan, J. V., Kaplan, A. G., Miller, J. B., Stiver, I. P., & Surrey, J. L. (1991). *Women's growth in connection: Writings from the Stone Center.* The Guilford Press.

Jordan, J. (1991). Empathy and self boundaries. In J. V. Jordan, A. G. Kaplan, J. B. Miller, I. P. Stiver, & J. L. Surrey (Eds.), *Women's growth in connection: Writings from the Stone Center* (pp. 67–80). The Guilford Press.

Kendi, I. X. (2019). *How to be an antiracist.* Random House.

Kushner, K. E., & Morrow, R. (2003). Grounded theory, feminist theory, critical theory: Toward theoretical triangulation. *Advances in Nursing Science, 26*(1), 30–43. https://doi.org/10.1097/00012272-200301000-00006

Ladkin, D. (2008). Leading beautifully: How mastery, congruence and purpose create the aesthetic of embodied leadership practice. *The Leadership Quarterly, 19*(1), 31–41. https://doi.org/10.1016/j.leaqua.2007.12.003

Ladkin, D. (2012). Perception, reversibility, "flesh": Merleau-Ponty's phenomenology and leadership as embodied practice. *Integral Leadership Review, 12*(1), 1–13. Retrieved from https://integralleadershipreview.com/6280-perception-reversibility-flesh-merleau-pontys-phenomenology-and-leadership-as-embodied-practice/

Lakoff, R. T. (2004). *Language and woman's place: Text and commentaries: Revised and expanded edition.* Oxford University Press.

Lawler, J., & Ashman, I. (2012). Theorizing leadership authenticity: A Sartrean perspective. *Leadership, 8*(4), 327–44. https://doi.org/10.1177/1742715012444685

Leder, D. (1990). *The absent body.* University of Chicago Press.

Lewis, P., & Simpson, R. (2010.) *Revealing and concealing gender: Issues of visibility in organizations.* Palgrave Macmillan.

Lightsey, P. (2015). *Our lives matter: A womanist queer theology.* Pickwick.

Lincoln, Y. S., & Guba, E. G. (2013). *The constructivist credo.* Left Coast Press. https://doi.org/10.4324/9781315418810

Liu, H., Cutcher, L., & Grant, D. (2015). Doing authenticity: The gendered construction of authentic leadership. *Gender, Work and Organization, 22*, 237–255. https://doi.org/10.1111/gwao.12073

Liu, H. (2020). *Redeeming leadership: An anti-racist feminist intervention.* Bristol University Press. https://doi.org/10.1332/policypress/9781529200041.001.0001

Longino, H. E. (2017). Feminist Epistemology. In J. Greco, & E. Sosa (Eds.), *The Blackwell guide to epistemology* (pp. 325–353). Blackwell. https://doi.org/10.1002/9781405164863.ch14

Marrone, J. A., Ferraro, H. S., & Huston, T. (2018). A theoretical approach to female team leaders' boundary work choices. *Group & Organization Management, 43*(5), 825–856. https://doi.org/10.1177/1059601118795384

Maynard, D. (2010). *When sheep attack.* CreateSpace Independent Publishing.

Merleau-Ponty, M. (1945/1974). *Phenomenology of perception.* Routledge & K. Paul; Humanities Press. https://doi.org/10.4324/9780203981139

McKinney, K. (2022). *Less of a balancing act and more of a juggling act: How women who work in student affairs and having children with disabilities navigate their dual roles.* [Doctoral dissertation, Rowan University].

Menakem, R. (2017). *My grandmother's hands: Racialized trauma and the pathway to mending our hearts and bodies.* Central Recovery Press.

Miller, S. H. (2013, May 23). Why we should be concerned that women remain outnumbered in theological education. *Christianity Today, 57*(4). Retrieved from https://www.christianitytoday.com/ct/2013/may-web-only/seminary-gender-gap.html

Moore, J. R. (2021). The frontier of race in mimetic theory: American lynchings and racial violence. *Contagion: Journal of Violence, Mimesis, and Culture, 28*(1), 1–31. https://doi.org/10.14321/contagion.28.2021.0001

Morris, K. J. (2012). *Starting with Merleau-Ponty.* Continuum International Pub. https://doi.org/10.5040/9781350251892

Mosley-Monts, A. (2022). *Demarginalizing Black Ordained Women's Voices in the Black Baptist Church: A Phenomenological Study of Black Women Ministers' Lived Experiences when Seeking Cleric Leadership Roles* (Publication No. 30240945) [Doctoral dissertation, University of Maryland]. ProQuest Dissertations & Theses.

Myers, L. (2020). *Female church leaders and compassion fatigue: A qualitative study.* (Publication No. 28029568) [Doctoral dissertation, Grand Canyon University]. ProQuest Dissertations Publishing.

Nagoski, E., & Nagoski, A. (2020). *Burnout: The secret of unlocking the stress cycle.* Ballatine.

Nagy Hesse-Biber, S., & Piatelli, D. (2014). The feminist practice of holistic reflexivity. In S. Nagy Hesse-Biber (Ed.) *Handbook of feminist research: Theory and praxis* (pp. 557–582). Sage. https://doi.org/10.4135/9781483384740.n27

Nast, H. (1992). Women in the field: Critical feminist methodologies and theoretical Perspectives. *Professional Geographer, 46*(1), 54–66. https://doi.org/10.1111/j.0033-0124.1994.00054.x

Norris, M. (2020, Dec 18). Don't call it a racial reckoning: The race toward equality has barely begun. *Washington Post.* Retrieved from https://www.washingtonpost.com/opinions/dont-call-it-a-racial-reckoning-the-race-toward-equality-has-barely-begun/2020/12/18/90b65eba-414e-11eb-8bc0-ae155bee4aff_story.html

Novak, S. (1994). The Girardian theory and feminism: Critique and appropriation. *Contagion: Journal of Violence, Mimesis, and Culture, 1,* 19–29. https://doi.org/10.1353/ctn.1994.0000

Office of the General Assembly, Presbyterian Church (U.S.A.). (2021). *Employment guidance for PC(USA) sessions and session personnel committees.* Retrieved from https://www.pcusa.org/site_media/media/uploads/oga/pdf/employment_guidance_for_sessions_and_session_personnel_committees_2021.pdf

O'Neill, C. E. (2018). Unwanted appearances and self-objectification: The phenomenology of alterity for women in leadership. *Leadership, 15*(3), 296–318. https://doi.org/10.1177/1742715018816561

Page, S. J. (2016). Altruism and sacrifice: Anglican priests managing 'intensive' priesthood and motherhood. *Religion and Gender, 6*(1), 47–63. https://doi.org/10.18352/rg.10127

Page, S., & McPhillips, K. (2021). Introduction: Religion, gender and violence. *Religion and Gender, 11*, 151–165. https://doi.org/10.1163/18785417-01102001

Pence, E., & McDonnell, C. (1984). *Power and control wheel.* Duluth, MN: Domestic Abuse Intervention Project. Retrieved from https://www.theduluthmodel.org/

Polka, W., Litchka, P., & Davis, S. W. (2008). Female superintendents and the professional victim syndrome: Preparing current and aspiring superintendents to cope and succeed. *Journal of Women in Educational Leadership, 6*(4), 293–311. Retrieved from https://core.ac.uk/download/pdf/33137758.pdf

Porges, S. W. (2011). *The polyvagal theory: Neurophysiological foundations of emotions, attachment, communication, and self-regulation.* W W Norton & Co.

Potapchuk, W. (1990). Processes of governance: Can governments truly respond to human needs. In J. Burton (Ed.) *Conflict: Human Needs Theory* (pp. 265–282) St. Martin's Press. https://doi.org/10.1007/978-1-349-21000-8_14

Public Religion Research Institute (2020). *The American religious landscape in 2020.* Retrieved from https://www.prri.org/research/2020-census-of-american-religion/#page-section-1

Redekop, V. (2002). *From violence to blessing: How an understanding of deep-rooted conflict can open paths to reconciliation.* Novalis.

Rediger, G.L. (1997). *Clergy killers: Guidance for pastors and congregations under attack.* Westminster John Knox Press.

Reineke, M. (1990). The devils are come down upon us": Myth, history and the witch as scapegoat, in A. Bach (Ed.), *The pleasures of her text, feminist readings of biblical and historical texts.* Trinity Press International. Retrieved from https://www.religion-online.org/book-chapter/chapter-7-the-devils-are-come-down-upon-us-myth-history-and-the-witch-as-scapegoat-by-martha-j-reineke/

Reineke, M. (1992). The Mother in Mimesis: Kristeva and Girard on Violence and the Sacred. In D. Crownfield (Ed.), *Body/text in Julia Kristeva : religion, women, and psychoanalysis* (pp. 67–85). State University of New York Press.

Reineke, M. (1997). *Sacrificed Lives: Kristeva on Women and Violence.* Indiana University.

Reineke, M. (2009). Sacrifice and sexual difference: Insights and challenges in the work of René Girard. In S. Goodhard, J. Jørgensen, T. Ryba, & J. Williams (Eds.), *For René Girard: Essays in Friendship and in Truth* (pp. 247–258). Michigan State University Press.

Reineke, M. (2014). *Intimate domain: Desire, Trauma, and mimetic theory.* Michigan State University Press.

Reiss, S. (2015). *The 16 strivings for god: The new psychology of religious experiences.* Mercer University Press.

Reynolds, K. (2014). Servant-leadership: A Feminist perspective. *The International Journal of Servant-Leadership, 10*(1), 35–63. https://doi.org/10.33972/ijsl.110

Rike, J. (1996). The cycle of violence and feminist constructions of selfhood. *Contagion: Journal of Violence, Mimesis, and Culture, 3,* 21–42. https://doi.org/10.1353/ctn.1996.0008

Roberts, R. (2016). Embodied leadership: Corporeal experiences of a female Anglican priest. In Flynn, P., Haynes, K., Kilgour, M, Roberts, R. (Eds.), *Overcoming challenges to gender equality in the workplace: Leadership and innovation* (pp. 78–94). Greenleaf. https://doi.org/10.9774/gleaf.9781783532667_8

Roberts, R. M. (2022). *Women seeking the public school superintendency: Navigating the gendered and racialized-gendered job search* [Doctoral dissertation, Antioch University] https://aura.antioch.edu/etds/861

Rocca, F. X. (2023, June 24). Southern Baptists Resoundingly Reject Women Pastors. *The Wall Street Journal.* Retrieved from https://www.wsj.com/articles/southern-baptists-confirm-rejection-of-women-pastors-6af4de3c

Rohrer, K. (2020). A small shift toward sharing all things common. In S. Hagley, K. Rohrer, & M. Gehrling, (Eds.), *Sustaining grace: Innovative ecosystems for new faith communities* (pp. 23–34). Wipf and Stock.

Ryan, M. K., & Haslam, S. A. (2005). The glass cliff: Evidence that women are over-represented in precarious leadership positions. *British Journal of Management, 16,* 81–90. https://doi.org/10.1111/j.1467-8551.2005.00433.x

Ryan, M. K., & Haslam, S. A. (2007). The glass cliff: Exploring the dynamics surrounding the appointment of women to precarious leadership positions. *Academy of Management Review 32*(2), 549–572. https://doi.org/10.5465/amr.2007.24351856

Schatzman, L. (1991). Dimensional analysis: Notes on an alternative approach to the grounding of theory in qualitative research. In D. R. Maines (Ed.), *Social organization and social process* (pp. 303–314). Aldine De Gruyter.

Schulz, J., Bahrami-Rad, D., Beauchamp, J., & Henrich, J. (June 22, 2018). The Origins of WEIRD Psychology. *Social Science Research Network.* https://doi.org/10.2139/ssrn.3201031

Schwartz, H. L. (2019). *Connected teaching: Relationship, power, and mattering in higher education.* Stylus Publishing, LLC.

Shoop, M. (2010). *Let the bones dance: Embodiment and the body of Christ.* Westminster John Knox Press.

Sinclair, A. (2005). Body possibilities in leadership. *Leadership, 1*(4), 387–406. https://doi.org/10.1177/1742715005057231

Sinclair, A. (2012) Leading with body. In E. Jeanes, D. Knights, & P.Y. Martin (Eds.), *Handbook of gender, work & organization* (pp. 117–30). Wiley.

Sinclair, A. (2013). Can I really be me? Challenges for women leaders constructing authenticity. In D. Ladkin & C. Spiller (Eds.), *Reflections on authentic leadership: Concepts, coalescences and clashes* (pp. 239–51). Edward Elgar. https://doi.org/10.4337/9781781006382.00029

Smith, M. K. (2015, March 17). *Presbyterian Church (U.S.A.) approves marriage amendment.* Retrieved from https://www.pcusa.org/news/2015/3/17/presbyterian-church-us-approves-marriage-amendment/

Stiver, I. (1986). *Beyond the oedipus complex: Mothers and daughters.* Wellesley Centers for Women. Retrieved from https://www.wcwonline.org/vmfiles/26sc.pdf

Strutzenberg, C. C., Wiersma-Mosley, J. D., Jozkowski, K. N., & Becnel, J. N. (2017). Love-bombing: A narcissistic approach to relationship formation. *Discovery, The Student Journal of Dale Bumpers College of Agricultural, Food and Life Sciences, 18*(1), 81–89.

Tanner, D. (2016, Mar 15). The self-fulfilling prophecy of disliking Hillary Clinton. *Time Magazine*. Retrieved from https://time.com/4258976/disliking-hillary-clinton/

The Pew Forum on Religion and Public Life (2011, March 31). Employment of clergy. In *Church in court: The legal status of religious organization in civil lawsuits*. Retrieved from https://www.pewresearch.org/religion/2011/03/31/churches-in-court3/

Torjesen, K. (1993). *When women were priests: Women's leadership in the early church and the scandal of their subordination in the rise of Christianity*. Harper.

Turner, J. (2015). The disenchantment of Western performance training and the search for an embodied experience: Toward a methodology of the ineffable In M. Perry & C.L. Medina, (Eds.), *Methodologies of embodiment: Inscribing bodies in qualitative research* (pp. 53–68). Routledge. https://doi.org/10.4324/9780203582190-4

Van der Kolk, B. A. (2014). *The body keeps the score: Brain, mind, and body in the healing of trauma*. Penguin Publishing Group.

Van Wijk-Bos, J. (2022). A squeegee in your path: Resisting erasure. In D. Meyers & M.S. Barnett (Eds.), *Hating Girls: An Intersectional Survey of Misogyny* (pp. 96–115). Haymarket. https://doi.org/10.1163/9789004467002_007

Walker, M. (2019). *When getting along is not enough: Reconstructing race in our lives and relationships*. Teachers College Press.

Watts, J. (2010). Now you see me, now you don't: The visibility paradox for women in a male-dominated profession. In P. Lewis & R. Simpson (Eds.), *Revealing and concealing gender: Issues of visibility in organizations* (pp. 175–193). Palgrave. https://doi.org/10.1057/9780230285576_10

Weber, M. (1963). *The sociology of religion*. Boston Beacon.

Weil, S. (1959). *Waiting for god*. (E. Craufurd, Trans.). Capricorn. (Original work published 1951). https://doi.org/10.4324/9781003146773

Weir, A. (1996) *Sacrificial logics: Feminist theory and the critique of identity*. Routledge. https://doi.org/10.4324/9781315865935

Williams, J. (1996). (Ed.). *The Girard Reader*. Crossroad Publishing.

Willis, R. (2019). The use of composite narratives to present interview findings. *Qualitative Research, 19*(4), 471–480. https://doi.org/10.1177/1468794118787711

Youngs, S. (2011, May 10) *Presbyterian Church (U.S.A.) approves change in ordination standard*. Retrieved from https://www.pcusa.org/news/2011/5/10/presbyterian-church-us-approves-change-ordination/

Zikmund, B., Lummis, A., & Chang, P. (1998). *Clergy women: An uphill calling*. Westminster John Knox Press.

www.ingramcontent.com/pod-product-compliance
Lightning Source LLC
Chambersburg PA
CBHW062128020426
42335CB00013B/1137

9 781966 655138